T0343552

Yes, Daddy!

A celebration of our favourite
internet Daddies

Illustrated by Jovilee Burton

SEVEN DIALS

First published in Great Britain in 2023 by Seven Dials,
an imprint of The Orion Publishing Group Ltd
Carmelite House, 50 Victoria Embankment
London EC4Y 0DZ

An Hachette UK Company

1 3 5 7 9 10 8 6 4 2

A CIP catalogue record for this book is
available from the British Library.

ISBN (Hardback) 978 1 3996 2012 3
ISBN (eBook) 978 1 3996 2013 0

Typeset by Goldust Design
Printed and bound in Great Britain by Clays Ltd, Elcograf S.p.A.

www.orionbooks.co.uk

To Internet Daddies and all who thirst for them

xxx

Contents

Introduction

Internet Daddy, *noun*
A Daddy is a male authority figure, typically older and definitely attractive. The term Daddy is a slang term of affection and adoration – not to be confused with your own paternal relation.

I know you've felt it. That deep yearning that tugs at your stomach and the desire that flushes through your body as you look upon a man, not just any man, but one with the effortless confidence that comes with age. His face is rugged and worn. He has experienced things. His hair and beard are peppered with grey, and his skin looks like it's seen outdoor work, hard outdoor work. The kind of work that is just so attractive when a man does it, like chopping logs, building fences or digging holes. The essential things that were once required to survive and that bring feral women out in droves.

The man's eyes lock with yours and the force of passion startles you. You somehow know immediately that he could do the car maintenance and take out the rubbish. He can create a plan and see it through, because he's done it so many times before. He's funny in a doesn't-take-life-too-seriously kind of way, a lovely silly and good-with-kids way. He's knowledgeable, but doesn't force it down your throat. Instead, he holds his wisdom like a wise old owl. If wise owls were sexy.

Just like a rich and full-bodied wine, these men have matured, refined and reached a whole new level of fine. They are fatherly in their temperament and more emotionally *developed* which means they are the opposite of the fuckbois that plague us all in the real world. Often, they are also fathers in real life, but that's not our business because the wife and kids tend to jar with our imaginations.

Internet Daddies embody the fantasies that keep our pulses racing and hearts pumping when often the realities of men and dating – and more specifically dating men – can be so disappointing, unromantic and unfulfilling. Fantasy is the most important and compelling word in this. These men have their true identities and then the ones we ascribe to them, they may not be anything like the people we create here. If these men are problematic at any time in the coming years – and as we know very well, the likelihood of that is high – they will be *removed* from future editions of this book. Only the best men deserve to be held up as Daddies.

Now, in our celebration of these worldly, rugged and emotionally mature men we are embracing the dreams that sustain us, and if dreaming was good enough for Martin Luther King, it's good enough for us (side note: MLK was a bit of a Daddy himself). This is a playful and joyful revelling in the female – and sometimes gays and theys – gaze, one where we can all be entertained by and laugh about our multi-faceted, emotionally charged desires. A small yet mighty book that holds a selection of meet-cutes where you are always the main character. In a world that prioritises male attraction and attention, we are shifting the dial and placing ourselves at the centre of the narrative. Women deserve to feel enveloped, cared for, listened to, considered, and we deserve someone who can lift some of the burdens we carry in this world where so many systems are set against us – bet you didn't think this book would be political, I contain multitudes, so think again. What we imagine in the men that we list in this book is someone who can do all the above but, most importantly, respects women, and what could be hotter than that?

If anything, this book should be considered a scientific analysis. Yep, I went there. It's a considered assessment of our yearning. A study of women's lust in all its manifestations. So, consider this a good use of your time! Within these pages,will be a unique, first-of-its-kind celebration of Zaddies (the supreme overlords of Daddies), Daddies and their . . . attributes, the ultimate scores of the defining Daddies of today. From Pedro Pascal to Oscar Isaac; Idris Elba to Jason Momoa and beyond, this will be your Daddy Bible. Will this book be unhinged? Absolutely yes. Do we all need attachment therapy? Definitely. But now's not the time for thinking of that. Instead, quench your thirst, release your guiltiest of desires and embrace your lust as we immerse ourselves in every rivet, curve and bristled surface of the Daddy. To the men we cover in this book: we appreciate you and the energy you inspire in us, thank you for your service.

Whether you received this as a gift, bought it for your personal collection, or even hate-purchased it, I hope you enjoy these moments to sit back, relax and delve into the wonders of the female mind.

Where men never, ever, *ever* disappoint.

Pedro Pascal

Señor Pascal shot to global fame through his roles as the Mandalorian, Javier Peña and Oberyn Martell. Since then, he has been making real strides towards becoming one of the best actors on screen, as well as rallying for the top job as Daddy Supreme.

Chilean-born and after nearly a decade of small roles, he's finally getting the recognition he deserves. He electrified many in his role as Joel Miller in *The Last of Us*, where he played the part of older man with the grumpy exterior and warm heart so perfectly, it was if he designed the trope himself. Many more films and TV shows will be starring Pascal in the coming years, so thankfully we'll be seeing much more of this rugged Latin Daddy.

As an LGBTQ+ advocate, technology-unsteady and all-round sweet man, he really takes the whole bakery when it comes to the wholesome, supportive and fatherly persona.

'Everyone thinks I'm some kind of athlete and I'm really not. I'm just an actor and my back is killing me.'

Pedro Pascal

OVERALL DADDY/ZADDY SCORE	99
ATTAINABILITY	95
LOVEABLENESS	98
ABILITY TO CHOP LOGS	52
DAD JOKE EXPERTISE	65
LEADERSHIP SKILLS (AIRPORT DAD MODE ACTIVATION)	89
FASHION FORWARDNESS	82

SPECIAL POWER?
Moustache

The LA skyline shimmers and dances in your view as you breathe in the humid air and absorb the city. You're on a work trip and you're feeling like a *boss*. You know you're looking fine because a kindly older lady complimented you earlier that day.

That night, you are attending a premiere for a film that has got all the critics talking. You were explicitly asked to come because you are just that well-known and respected. You're excited, but in a low-key, you've-done-this-a-million-times-before kind of way. You've tried on the dress. A silky backless, figure-hugging piece that skims over each curve and hugs every inch like it was designed specifically for you. Maybe it was – you're incredibly rich. Your make-up is done perfectly, and you have that skinny feeling that you get in the morning sometimes. The world isn't ready for you.

On the red carpet, cameras are flashing, and you smile broadly knowing that you are a mystery to these people, an enticing mystery. Everyone is doing a double take to get a proper look at you as you glow and glisten in the bright lights. As you head into the bar area, you feel a large, strong hand hold your wrist and you turn in surprise as the person, in a voice as deep and smooth as hot chocolate, says, 'Hey, I've wanted to meet you forever! Forgive me but, I must say, *eres hermosa y impresionante*.'

Pedro Pascal's eyes crinkle up into a smile, his eyes squinting as he takes in every inch of you. Immediately you can speak fluent Spanish.

'*Mucho gusto, señor*.' You smile subtly. It's effortless, and Pedro raises his eyebrows . . .

'*Hablas Español*? Wow, I love that. I'm Pedro by the way, I meant to say.' He seemed shy, was he . . . nervous?

Your eyes graze over him. He's wearing a blazer and trousers and his shirt is open to reveal a silver medallion nestled in a chest that puffs out with confidence, dark hairs swirling flirtatiously down to where the shirt buttons begin. He seems friendly but unknowable, cuddly but perhaps slightly dangerous. He exudes a humbleness and a sex appeal that would knock most women to the ground in a fit of giggles in an instant, but you are not most women.

'I'm the one at the premiere for *your* film I should be the one coming over to say I've been wanting to meet you!' You say playfully.

'I'm not all that.' He chuckles. 'You're the one setting the world alight with your scripts. I was sent your recent one today. Incredible. The depth to the comedy and the romance is like nothing I've read before. I just hope I get the casting.'

You blush in what you hope isn't noticeable, but from the way his smile widens, you can see it is.

'Well, thank you very much. If I'm honest, I'd love for you to play the lead.'

Pedro clutches his hand to his heart. 'You're kidding?! You have just made my whole night and it's only just begun. And I think . . . ' his gaze assesses every soft curve and arch of your body, 'I *know* it can only get better from here.'

You lean in, your fingers graze his, and his eyes widen in pleasant surprise. 'If you play your cards right, I think it will.'

The premiere continues and wherever Pedro is in the room you can feel his eyes follow you. As you speak to the other stars, to the director and writers and producers, as you catch his eye from the audience and feel your heart pounding in your chest.

Once you've done the dance of moving around each other, in each other's orbits but never quite meeting, he makes purposeful steps towards you.

'I'm no good at bluffing, and I've never been good at keeping my cards close to my chest. I really, *really* want to take you out of here and continue our conversation.' He runs his hand down your forearm.

You laugh, 'That's exactly what I was hoping you'd say.'

Pedro places a hand on the small of your back and you walk out of the room as whispers build around you both. This will be the talk of inner circles for a good week. But you don't care, as you leave the event, a fire building in your stomach and travelling to your cheeks, you know you've scored a full house and that tonight might be the first night of the rest of your life.

Óscar Isaac

Óscar Isaac Hernández Estrada is another fine ass Latinx man on a compelling mission to make all the women and men of the world fall in love with him. He is relentless in this mission in fact.

Óscar was born in Guatemala but his family moved to the US when he was young. Today he is one of the best actors in the world, credited with breaking stereotypes for Latinx characters in Hollywood and named one of the twenty-five greatest actors of the twenty-first-century by the *New York Times* in 2020. He has truly brought new life to a number of alieny space film brands including *Star Wars* and *X-Men*. He also set pulses racing in his role as a titular superhero in *Moon Knight*.

He is an actor who has the good looks and the charisma, the sweetest smile and affable demeanour but he is also someone who is contagiously passionate about his art, and because of this he is completely and utterly convincing in the roles he plays.

'I think it's good to be a little more fearless in saying what you feel.'

DADDY SCORE

Óscar Isaac

OVERALL DADDY/ZADDY SCORE	83
ATTAINABILITY	22
LOVEABLENESS	85
ABILITY TO CHOP LOGS	75
DAD JOKE EXPERTISE	22
LEADERSHIP SKILLS (AIRPORT DAD MODE ACTIVATION)	65
FASHION FORWARDNESS	60

SPECIAL POWER?
Ability to Grow a Strong Beard.

Colin Firth

Famous English actor Colin Firth is the pinnacle of stability, security and consistency, and in a world where men love to let you down, there is something distinctly attractive about that. Colin seized hearts in his roles as Mr Darcy in *Pride and Prejudice*, Mark Darcy in *Bridget Jones's Diary* and Harry in *Mamma Mia!* He has even been awarded a CBE for his services to drama. Now the founder of Raindog Films, he works as a producer and his films have grossed more than $3 billion worldwide – yes, girls, he's got money.

His parents are academics, and Colin himself has even researched and written an academic paper in the field of political neuroscience. It's the smart and handsome combination that comes together like the finest wine and cheese pairing. On top of this, he puts this knowledge to great use, as a campaigner for asylum seekers, refugees' rights, the rights of indigenous people and the environment.

'Because I am an Englishman I spend most of my life in a state of embarrassment.'

DADDY SCORE

Colin Firth

OVERALL DADDY/ZADDY SCORE	51
ATTAINABILITY	23
LOVEABLENESS	84
ABILITY TO CHOP LOGS	47
DAD JOKE EXPERTISE	33
LEADERSHIP SKILLS (AIRPORT DAD MODE ACTIVATION)	67
FASHION FORWARDNESS	52

SPECIAL POWER?
Gentlemanly Britishness

Mads Mikkelsen

Mads Mikkelsen sits in the minority group of men who are both scary but also very sexy. His dark, mysterious and brooding energy is unsettling – in a seductive way – and is probably a big reason why he has played some of the most iconic villains in pop culture history. It's quite funny to learn that the Danish actor started off as a skilled gymnast and dancer, in fact he was a professional dancer for a decade before he turned his hand to acting. It was his role as Le Chiffre in the twenty-first James Bond film, *Casino Royale*, that propelled him into worldwide recognition and crowned him the antagonist of the century. Since then, he has played iconic and sociopathic characters such as Dr Hannibal Lecter, Kaecilius and Gellert Grindelwald. I believe Hollywood is missing a trick in not casting Mads in a romantic comedy as either the serious and misunderstood Scandinavian heir or a mysterious lumberjack. If you're a producer reading this, you know what you have to do.

'I like to stay home with my family. But travel is good in a way. It makes you redefine each other each time you see each other. Also, it helps that I think my wife is the hottest woman in the world.'

Mads Mikkelsen

OVERALL DADDY/ZADDY SCORE	95
ATTAINABILITY	-20 (this man *loves* his wife)
LOVEABLENESS	10
ABILITY TO CHOP LOGS	70
DAD JOKE EXPERTISE	10
LEADERSHIP SKILLS (AIRPORT DAD MODE ACTIVATION)	85
FASHION FORWARDNESS	75

SPECIAL POWER?
Villainy

The library has emptied over the course of the day, and you can see the sun setting through the high windows, the light refracting through the stained glass. The musty smell of books lingers around you, and you shiver at the eeriness of being alone in such an ancient space. You pluck a book from the shelf and head back to where you have been working on your first book, the space reflecting the bustling intensity of your mind.

You sit down and open the book, delving into these new expansive worlds and histories illustrated for you by authors of times past – likely authors who had sat in this very library and looked up to this same ornate ceiling. As you take a breath and look around, the air catches in your lungs. Across from you, down one of the aisles, is a man who is reading a book intently.

Your heart pumps in your chest as you assess him, noticing that he seems to not have noticed you. Not wanting to give him a fright, you cough lightly so he can sense your presence. He looks towards you briefly, eyebrows raised in surprise. You smile at each other, and to your surprise he walks over.

As he does so, you take a moment to appraise him. His eyes have a lightness to them that is compelling, and his jaw is sharp. He has a face that is slightly disconcerting while also eye-catching, and he is enveloped in a mysteriousness that fills you with curiosity.

'My apologies, I didn't mean to disturb you or frighten you. I've seen you before, but I notice you usually sit over the other side. I try not to bother you as it can feel a bit eerie in here in the evenings.'

His demeanour is friendly but reserved. He seems genuinely apologetic. You're shocked that you've never noticed him before.

'That's . . . it's no problem, really. I moved over here to be nearer the books I needed. I'm equally sorry to have disturbed you.'

He nods calmly. 'What are you working on? If you don't mind me asking.'

The mess of papers and books that surrounds you seems distinctly more chaotic through his eyes.

'I'm writing a book.'

His face gives very little away. 'Is that right? You seem to be reading more books than writing.'

You are taken aback. 'I think, I guess I get distracted. There are so many brilliant minds to read, I feel like I need to consider them all to hopefully be able to match them with my own work. You know, in the Renaissance times, wealthy men used to spend years of their lives reading, considering art in all of its forms and experiencing different cultures before they started to create their own art. I would love to do that. If it weren't for deadlines, and bills.'

You don't know why you just opened up like that to this total stranger, but something about his brooding smile and his presence made you want to submit to him completely.

'"Sail while the breeze blows. Wind and tide wait for no man."'

'Sorry?'

'It means you should go where inspiration takes you, where nature guides you. It's about following your intuition and your heart. Life has a way of guiding you in the direction you were always meant to go.' He sits down beside you. And you are caught up again in those light eyes. He continues, 'Perhaps part of nature guiding you is meeting a stranger in the library who encourages you to use your brilliant mind, to take your time and write from your soul.'

'Perhaps.' You gulp.

He picks up the book you had been reading intently just moments before. 'These men, they only knew so much of the world. You, you have a unique perspective and viewpoint they will never possess, and you should feel confident in that.'

He lays the book down and brushes your arm. He gets up and heads back to where he came from.

'My name is Mads. I hope we will meet again. I believe we will. The breeze seems to keep blowing me towards you, no matter what I do.'

You nod. Dumbstruck. 'I hope so too.'

He shoots you a smile that seems to contain a million different possibilities. And then, he fades away into the books, just as the last inch of light disappears from the library windows.

Daniel Dae Kim

Daniel Dae Kim. Even his name is hot. This American actor was born in South Korea and moved to the US when he was only one. He began his career on stage, and despite his early success he decided to deepen his knowledge of the acting craft and attained a master's from New York University's Graduate Acting Program. It was following this that he truly launched his film and TV career.

You may know him from his role as Jin-Soo Kwon in *Lost* or Chin Ho Kelly on *Hawaii Five-O*, or maybe Jack Kang in the *Divergent* films. His various and multifaceted roles have landed him worldwide acclaim and he has been individually honoured with an AZN Asian Excellence Award, a Multicultural Prism Award and a Vanguard Award from the Korean American Coalition, all for Outstanding Performance by an Actor.

As well as his career in performance and acting, he actively pursues interests in the community at large, having served as Cultural Envoy and Member of the US Presidential Delegation for the United States at the World Expo in South Korea. And beyond this, he spearheads his own production company, 3AD. Ambitious, bold and talented, with a face and body that may as well have been carved by the hands of Venus herself, it seems like there may be nothing this man cannot do.

Daniel Dae Kim

OVERALL DADDY/ZADDY SCORE	85
ATTAINABILITY	-3
LOVEABLENESS	92
ABILITY TO CHOP LOGS	99
DAD JOKE EXPERTISE	35
LEADERSHIP SKILLS (AIRPORT DAD MODE ACTIVATION)	76
FASHION FORWARDNESS	63

SPECIAL POWER?
Could cut his enemies in half with his cheekbones

Paul Rudd

There is something about Paul Rudd. He might be a short king at five-foot-ten, but he is a short king with the comedy of one of the greatest fools in the kingdom. And if you know women, you know humour goes a long way. In fact, it was only in 2021 that *People* magazine named him the Sexiest Man Alive.

Paul Stephen Rudd has English parents who descend from Ashkenazi Jewish immigrants. The author notes that his mum lives down the road from her hometown, and the author is glad. He grew up in Kansas and studied at the American Academy of Dramatic Arts in New York before he appeared in the comedy film *Clueless* alongside Alicia Silverstone. It was through that role, his one in *Friends* and in *Anchorman* that he came to be known as the unlikely heart-throb of a generation.

Paul Rudd knows where the fountain of fineness is and he has definitely been drinking it by the gallon because even as he approaches older beekeeping age he is becoming more attractive than he has ever been. He is married, *sobs*, and lives happily with his wife and two children in New York.

If he ever wants to be reconnected to his British roots, all I'm saying is I'd be happy to cook him up a roast anytime.

'Look at us. Who'd have thought? Not me!'

DADDY SCORE

Paul Rudd

OVERALL DADDY/ZADDY SCORE	75
ATTAINABILITY	1
LOVEABLENESS	99
ABILITY TO CHOP LOGS	25
DAD JOKE EXPERTISE	100
LEADERSHIP SKILLS (AIRPORT DAD MODE ACTIVATION)	50
FASHION FORWARDNESS	40

SPECIAL POWER?
Comedy

TRANSCRIPT_version1_interview_Paul Rudd_deletedsection.docx

Journalist (you): We are here at the launch of the *Clueless* sequel with comedy extraordinaire, master of aging like a fine wine and fellow Brit, Paul Rudd. Hi Paul Rudd.

Paul Rudd: [smiling] Well, hey.

Journalist: How does it feel to be back in London town?

Paul Rudd: Like I never left. They brought out all of the fanfare upon my arrival.

Journalist: As they should. Had you missed the English breakfast?

Paul Rudd: I'll tell you what, I have really missed an English breakfast. Americans simply don't understand the wondrous delicacy that is baked beans.

Journalist: You haven't really lived until you've sampled a likkle baked bean on toast.

Paul Rudd: You make it sound so saucy.

Journalist: Famously, it is.

Paul Rudd: [laughs]

Journalist: How was it, coming back to the *Clueless* universe again after so long?

Paul Rudd: Now why the emphasis on the *so*? I'm not that old.

Journalist: I mean, the character does pay taxes, has multiple kids and a healthy retirement pot but sure, we'll take the emphasis away.

Paul Rudd: [chuckles] I've lost all hope that you might be flirting with me now.

Journalist: [laughs] Nothing sexier than a stable man with a significant retirement fund.

Paul Rudd: You're right. That's hot. I like that. But back to your question, reprising these classic cult-favourite films is *obviously* so much more than a capitalist money grab.

Journalist: [blushes] *Obviously*.

Paul Rudd: Emphasis required there.

Journalist: For sure.

Paul Rudd: [laughs] But I really did love bringing back Josh. He's more seasoned, he knows himself, he's grown in his independence. More than anything though, I needed the job.

Journalist: You're really going for the radical honesty here aren't you?

Paul Rudd: [laughs] For some reason, you seem to bring it out of me. In fact, you're making me a little bit nervous here, which is unacceptable given I'm the multi-award-winning celebrity.

Journalist: Paul Rudd, ladies and gents, honest *and* humble.

[Both laugh]

Journalist: I'll join in with the radical honesty. You are my celebrity crush.

[Paul fakes falling off his chair]

Paul Rudd: You can't be for real?

Journalist: Of course, I am! Serious as the plague.

Paul Rudd: We're going to need to start this interview again, aren't we? [Laughs]

Journalist: I would say so.

Paul Rudd: Drink after?

Journalist: Drink after.

[ENDS]

Henry Cavill

Henry William Dalgliesh Cavill is a British actor known for his portrayals of Superman, the Witcher and Sherlock Holmes. Unsurprisingly, he has been named the sexiest man alive in a number of magazines and it's true that this man probably couldn't get more traditionally handsome. He's like Prince Charming if Prince Charming never skipped leg day.

Born in Jersey, he now resides in South Kensington where he passes his time practising Brazilian jiu-jitsu, gaming (*World of Warcraft* is one of his favourites) and supporting conservation charities.

What's next for this Daddy's career is still to be seen, although he apparently gave a showstopping audition to be the next James Bond, it sounds like he hasn't been cast for the role to the woe of thirsty women and men everywhere.

'I'm loyal to a fault. I may have learned that from my mother.'

DADDY SCORE

Henry Cavill

OVERALL DADDY/ZADDY SCORE	98
ATTAINABILITY	40
LOVEABLENESS	10
ABILITY TO CHOP LOGS	100
DAD JOKE EXPERTISE	8
LEADERSHIP SKILLS (AIRPORT DAD MODE ACTIVATION)	98
FASHION FORWARDNESS	100

SPECIAL POWER?
Could accidentally push you over and you'd say 'thank you'

n one of the most beautiful hotels in Mayfair, you stand by the bar with a vodka martini. Eyes are drawn to you as you move with ease and the waiter serves you eagerly, a hopeful glint in his eye.

That is until someone taps you on the shoulder and kisses the soft part of your neck.

'You look incredible.'

You turn and see Henry, in a suit with a shirt that opens at the neck and gives a glimpse of his muscular chest. He has sunglasses on inside which would seem arrogant for most men, but on him looks totally normal. If normal was to be the most good-looking man you'd ever laid your eyes upon.

You'd dated Henry at university when you were young and carefree, downing vodbulls in pulsating clubs, your feet sticking to the floor. You'd stumble home together in the early hours, as the birds sang out in the sky and the sun's heat had already begun to warm the pavements. After university, you'd gone your separate ways, each of you seeking to find your independence and learn more about yourself.

It was only last month when Henry had reached out to you to reconnect. He was now a successful actor, oozing with the confidence and wealth that came with being the face of a global franchise and the confidence of being widely known as one of the sexiest men alive. He wore it lightly, and it didn't seem to fill him with the self-importance it did some men. Instead, it gave him a steadiness and a self-assuredness.

He'd told you he was looking for something real. Something like you'd shared when you chain-smoked cigarettes on some friend's balcony in the small hours and intertwined every inch of your souls, hopes, dreams in the soft daze of twilight.

So now here you both are, reconnecting. And you are enjoying every single part of what that involved. You are rediscovering each other, learning what it means to be together as fully grown adults who carry more wisdom and resilience. He was giving you everything you could hope for from a man. He spoiled you with gifts, showered you with praise and dedicated his passions to making sure you were *satisfied* in every single way possible.

He adores how you delight in him. In his hand on your thigh as you drive to an event. In his words that never fail to tell you how special you are. In the way he introduces you with the highest praise. In the way he commands you to strip out of your dress. In the way he takes his time, to explore you and dive deep.

When you turn round and kiss him deeply, his eyes light up in surprise. The waiter turns away, bereft. People turn to look at you together.

'Oh,' his voice a deep, gruff symphony in your ears. 'I don't think you're ready to leave yet.'

Your lips curve up, knowingly. 'Definitely not.'

His hand grips yours. 'Let's go.'

He leads you away from the bar, into the lift that heads back up to the room you are sharing.

You stand patiently, but as soon as the lift doors close you pounce on each other. You feel his arms grip your waist tightly as your lips enmesh and he pushes you against the lift wall. Your hands caress his wide back and the muscles that are evident through the tailoring of his suit. The passion sends you both into a frenzy but when the doors ping open you push apart and pretend the heat between you is a fantasy. No one is outside the lift, and you laugh together, him pulling you in for a tender kiss before you head back to the room.

As he pushes the door open to lead you in, he turns and, as if reading your mind, says, 'I'm so glad to have met you all over again. This is beyond my wildest dreams.'

You reach up to put a hand to his face, his stubble tickling your hand. 'I had a feeling we'd find our way back to each other.'

Idris Elba

Idrissa Akuna Elba is an actor, producer, writer, DJ and music artist all wrapped into one delightful package of fine. No stranger to hard work, Idris gained a place in the National Youth Music Theatre with a Prince's Trust grant and to support himself between roles he worked as tyre-fitter, cold-caller and nightclub DJ under the name Big Driis. He secured his first roles in soap operas in 1997 and 1998 and continued on to be a notable name in UK television. It was his role as DCI John Luther that sent Idris' career stratospheric and from there, he secured roles in some of the biggest films including *Thor*, *Star Trek Beyond* and *Prometheus*. He has also been a voice actor in *Zootropolis*, *Finding Dory* and *The Jungle Book*. His accolades and awards keep coming and as well as a Golden Globe and Emmy, he has an OBE and has been named as both one of the most influential people in the world as well as one of the sexiest. He also won a 'Rear of the Year' award in 2017. You read that correctly. His charitable work is something to be admired as he works to bring attention to key issues in West Africa, as well as highlight key cultural contributions of people from African descent, just like himself.

'My definition of bad ass is that I'm a force of nature and a true spirit.'

Idris Elba

OVERALL DADDY/ZADDY SCORE	93
ATTAINABILITY	-40
LOVEABLENESS	98
ABILITY TO CHOP LOGS	100
DAD JOKE EXPERTISE	52
LEADERSHIP SKILLS (AIRPORT DAD MODE ACTIVATION)	84
FASHION FORWARDNESS	75

SPECIAL POWER?
DJ and rap ability

Jamie Foxx

Jamie Foxx, born Eric Marlon Bishop, may as well have invented cool. He could also have invented what it means to be multi-talented. From the age of five he was playing piano and at high school he became a quarterback, which he was so skilled at that he got press in Dallas newspapers.

In Hollywood, he gained prominence in his roles in *Dreamgirls*, *Horrible Bosses*, *Ray*, *Just Mercy*, *Django Unchained*, *The Amazing Spider-Man 2* and many, many more. With his incredible acting alone, he has scooped up most of the awards out there including an Academy Award, a BAFTA, a Golden Globe and a Screen Actors Guild Award.

But he doesn't stop there. Foxx is also a Grammy-Award winning musician, producing four albums and two number-one singles. Just recently, he added bestselling author to his accolades, as he published his memoir *Act Like You Got Some Sense*. Behind the scenes he is a caring father and family man.

'If I were an animal, I would be an eagle.'

DADDY SCORE

Jamie Foxx

OVERALL DADDY/ZADDY SCORE	89
ATTAINABILITY	80
LOVEABLENESS	35
ABILITY TO CHOP LOGS	66
DAD JOKE EXPERTISE	97
LEADERSHIP SKILLS (AIRPORT DAD MODE ACTIVATION)	88
FASHION FORWARDNESS	87

SPECIAL POWER?
Plays piano (hot)

You sit in a jazz bar talking and laughing with your friends. You require a stiff drink because very soon you will be called up on stage to sing for the first time. Your stomach flips and turns with each minute that brings you closer to the performance you have been working towards for half of your life. Anyone who is anyone is there tonight. Record label executives, managers, celebrities, artists, publicists. If there was ever a time to shine, it would be now.

You step up onto the stage and the pianist smiles at you warmly as he asks if you're ready.

'Ready as I'll ever be,' I respond.

The bright stage lights blind you and you are grateful because now you cannot see the hundred or so faces looking up at you, analysing your every move.

'Hi, everyone.' The sound of your voice shocks you for a second. 'I'm going to sing for you tonight, I hope you enjoy it, I hope it makes you think of all the good memories and that you take something away from it. Let's go.' You nod at the pianist and your nerves dissipate into the air as the sound of the music floods over you.

You grip the mic tighter and when the cue comes your voice pours out. You can sense the crowd warming to you and you can hear the odd noise of appraisal as you build towards the crescendo. When you reach the high note and hit it with ease, you know everyone is locked in, eyes on you. Everyone's living in the moment and the bar feels like the only possible place to be in the world that night.

You sing another song, and now the audience are clapping, dancing, moving with you, with each other. As you finish, you see a figure move up to the stage. For a second you think it might be security checking something, and then he moves into the light. You reckon you might pass out there and then because who walks onto the stage other than *the* Jamie Foxx?

He boldly saunters up to the pianist, shakes his hand and asks, 'May I?' And the pianist accepts, giving a knowing eyebrow raise to you before he moves off stage. You laugh into the mic and say, 'Please can you all give Jamie Foxx a warm welcome.'

Jamie's deep brown eyes are full of cheekiness and mischief, and you match his energy in turn. He tells you what song he'd like you both to do and you gesture for him to go ahead.

It is completely off-the-cuff and unrehearsed but somehow the two of you together create magic. He is effortlessly talented with the piano, his fingers moving deftly across the keys, and when you reach the chorus, he starts to harmonise with you, your voices melding together in a delicious blend like milk and coffee. The crowd is beside itself at this point. Art is being created in front of them and they can all see the chemistry bonds being formed between the pair of you. One thing about passion is it's contagious and when you see one person enjoy their moment entirely uninhibited, it gives others the permission to do so too.

You reach the end of the song and Jamie comes to stand next to you, taking your hand in his, and you both bow to the cheers and whoops of the audience.

He doesn't let go of your hand as you walk off the stage and as you make your way to the backstage area. You are both giddy with excitement and as soon as you are out of sight, he turns to you, takes your other hand and says, 'That was amazing. *You* are amazing. I hope you didn't mind me coming up there, I just, I desperately wanted to play for you after hearing your voice.'

You feel like your brain has emptied of every possible thought or concept. There is nothing in your mind and body other than a buzzing of energy, excitement and desire. This is *Jamie Foxx* telling you *you* are talented. Totally and completely surreal, you squeeze his hands and whisper, 'I loved it, thank you.'

He gently leans in and kisses your cheek. Without realising, your bodies seem to have moved closer to each other like there is some magnet pulling you together, like they were always destined to touch.

Before it can go any further, your friends burst in and pour their congratulations, love and support over you. You hug them all and revel in the moment as they tell you how many people are ready to sign you, to manage you and to become your number one fans. Jamie has stepped to one side, but watches the scene in front of him calmly and coolly. He introduces himself to your friends with a respectful distance and he seems warm and interested in each one of them which you adore. He steps back and throws his hands up, 'I'm getting you all a drink.' And before you all know it he is back with the finest Dom Pérignon.

Your glass keeps getting refilled with champagne and you take a moment to sit down after circulating and talking to various important people all night.

'I hope you're soaking it all in.'

You look up and Jamie is there. He's leant back against the mahogany sofa, arm up on the ledge. His suppled body speaks of a confidence few possess but many desire.

'I think I've soaked up too much champagne, for sure.'

'And you should. This is your night. I am honoured to have been a small part of it.'

You're feeling brave so you move in closer to him and breathe, 'I feel like we didn't finish our part of the night.'

For the first time, this cool, calm, collected man seems a bit thrown. 'I wasn't sure if you were feeling it like that . . . I thought, damn, how can I meet this beautiful girl who is clearly charismatic, kind *and* talented and let her slip through my fingers? But I didn't want to distract from your moment. Still don't. So, if I'm overstepping, you just have to say . . . man, I usually have more game than this.' He rubs his hand down his face, exasperated but laughing and you laugh with him.

'I appreciate you letting me have my moment to shine, I really do. Maybe we can revisit this another time, and you can bring this game you speak of?' You place a hand on his and you can feel the hair on the back of your arm stand up on end.

He chuckles, sighs and leans into your ear, 'You're killing me, you know that? How about tomorrow, can we revisit then?'

You turn, eyes on his full lips, kissing them gently before saying, 'Tomorrow it is.'

You head back to your night, the night that changes everything, the night you've been waiting for . . . and you don't look back.

Jason Momoa

Jason Momoa, the man that you are.

Joseph Jason Namakaeha Momoa was born in Honolulu, Hawaii and is the miraculous creation of a photographer and a painter. And it was in Hawaii that he landed his first lead role in the TV show *Baywatch*, beating thousands of hopefuls in the process.

Most of us will have become aware of Mr Momoa through his role as Khal Drogo in *Game of Thrones*. How could we forget the blistering masculinity of the Dothraki king even though he only appeared in two seasons? That's impact, ladies and gentlemen. He has taken on major roles in Hollywood since then, including Conan the Barbarian and Aquaman, seizing a million hearts in the process.

Staying true to his rugged look, he apparently enjoys rock and ice climbing, mountain biking, snowboarding and skateboarding and apparently in his mid-teens he became the youngest lifeguard in the history of the Gulf Coast.

We hope to see much more of this man on our screens, and if not there, then could I just bump into him at some point? Much obliged.

'I think a man needs to be a man. To hold a woman the way she wants to be held. Just do whatever your woman wants, and you'll be fine.'

DADDY SCORE

Jason Mamoa

OVERALL DADDY/ZADDY SCORE (off the scale)	120+
ATTAINABILITY	90
LOVEABLENESS	83
ABILITY TO CHOP LOGS	110
DAD JOKE EXPERTISE	23
LEADERSHIP SKILLS (AIRPORT DAD MODE ACTIVATION)	99
FASHION FORWARDNESS (no need for fashion when you look that good in speedos.)	15

SPECIAL POWER?
Tall and big

You swim in an azure blue sea. This is the kind of blue the poets spoke of. 'A perfect shade of blue / to call my own.'[1] And as the late beams of the sun light up your face, you feel completely relaxed and totally at one with the world around you.

This private beach is totally secluded and at this time of the day, it feels like no one else exists on the island except you. And this is why you are startled by the man walking his dog along the shore. The sharp bark wakes you from your daze and you stand in the water and turn to look. You push your hair back and sigh, affronted, as the dog seems determined to come and say hello to you.

All this time you haven't looked up at the man once.

You walk towards the beach and the dog quickly comes up to greet you, and you must admit, he is adorable. His ears are soft as you pet him, and his tail wags with joy at your attention.

It is in that moment, you hear a deep voice say, 'I'm sorry about him!' and you decide to look up to the dog's owner for the first time. From your crouched position you turn your face upwards and realise you haven't looked high up enough as your eyes hit bare, chiselled, chest. You are startled and stand up quickly, and with your head almost tilted up to the sky to see the bearded, rugged, six-foot-four man stood before you. In that moment you decide the azure blue has found its competition in beauty. Or perhaps, this is the sea god who created a blue so beautiful.

'It's no trouble!' Your voice sounds painfully squeaky as you try to suppress the nerves bubbling in your chest.

1 Gainor Ventresco, 'A Perfect Shade of Blue'.

'He just loves making friends.' He laughs, patting his dog's head.

Your heart palpitates.

'Is that right?'

'I mean he *does* seem particularly inclined to make friends with beautiful women, but I'm not complaining about that.'

You look down at the dog who looks lovingly in your direction, and say to him, 'So you do this with most girls on the beach then? Damn, I thought I was special.' You look back at the owner/sea god/man of your dreams. 'What's his name?'

Sea god grins, 'Koa.'

'Koa's a flirt.'

'He is.'

Koa runs off into the sea, splashing around, excited to play and continue on his walk, but the sea god seems reluctant to leave. 'So, what brings you here? My name's Jason by the way.'

'A break from everyday life, I guess. Trying to see what it means not to be stuck in the hamster wheel of corporate life. Turns out, it's pretty lovely. It's nice to meet you.'

'Well, this is definitely the place for that. In fact, this is one of my favourite beaches on the island. It feels like it was designed by Pele herself.'

'Who is Pele?'

'Pele is the creator of the islands. A beautiful woman, strong in her emotions and her will to create,' he nods appraisingly at you. 'Not unlike yourself.'

You fear your knees might give way and if they do, you hope Koa might be there to catch you. Jason smiles knowingly at you. Oh he *knows* what he's doing to you and he loves it. 'I wonder if you might join me for dinner and a dance tonight? I'd love to show you more of this place, show you what being away from the corporate world can truly mean.'

The sea and sky seem to sing their approval at your union, the setting sun lights up the blue with oranges, purples and pinks. The poets had also spoken of meetings like this. The moment your soul intertwines with another and all the potential of laughs shared, kisses melted into skin, caresses lighting up the mind and body, just waiting to be made into reality. 'Apparently two, but one in soul, you and I.' Rumi spoke of this.

Emboldened by his invitation, his warm smile and the approval of the nature around you, you place your hand in his and say, 'We can start now if you like?'

Koa barks happily and bounds away in front of you as you walk along the long beach, the sun setting on the day, leaving a blank slate for a new union to rise the next morning.

George Clooney

The classic Daddy was brought up in Kentucky, with his first major role on *ER* (1994) as the sexy Dr Doug Ross making him a household name. The success of the *Ocean's Eleven, Twelve* and *Thirteen* franchise sits next to an Oscar for Best Supporting Actor and a Golden Globe. He has also seen success in directing and producing and was nominated for Best Director for *Good Night, and Good Luck* (2005). In 2023, Clooney became one of two people to have been nominated for Academy Awards in six different categories, a position he shares only with Walt Disney.

It is in his humanitarian work that George has really shown himself to be a proper well-rounded human, organising the Hope for Haiti telethon and being arrested while protesting at the Sudanese Embassy in Washington, D.C. He speaks out for gun control, LGBTQ+ rights and actively supported Barack Obama's presidential campaigns. His even more impressive wife, Amal Clooney, is a human rights lawyer, all-round incredible person and was named *Time* magazine's Woman of the Year in 2022. Together, they advocate for causes across the world for important causes.

'Failures are infinitely more instructive than successes.'

DADDY SCORE

George Clooney

OVERALL DADDY/ZADDY SCORE	60
ATTAINABILITY (We could *never* and would *never* try to compete with Amal Clooney)	-50
LOVEABLENESS	99
ABILITY TO CHOP LOGS	37
DAD JOKE EXPERTISE	25
LEADERSHIP SKILLS **(AIRPORT DAD MODE ACTIVATION)**	88
FASHION FORWARDNESS	73
SPECIAL POWER? Advocacy	

Keanu Reeves

Keanu Reeves, AKA the kindest man in Hollywood™, and perhaps one of the most well-known introverts, is a Canadian actor, born in Beirut and raised in Toronto. Over the years he has become a cult phenomenon through his performances in films such as *Youngblood, Bill & Ted's Excellent Adventure, Point Break* and *Speed*. He reached greater stardom with his role as Neo in the masterpiece that is *The Matrix*.

For a while, we didn't see much of our wholesome meme king, but he made a successful comeback with the *John Wick* film series, beginning in 2014, and in 2022 *Time* named him one of the most influential people in the world.

He has found new love since losing his long-term partner in 2001 and continues to bring love and advocacy into all his work. An all-round good guy, he has donated millions to charity and also has a substance deadly to fungi named after him: Keanumycin.

'If you have been brutally broken but still have the courage to be gentle to other living beings, then you're a badass with a heart of an angel.'

Keanu Reeves

OVERALL DADDY/ZADDY SCORE	92
ATTAINABILITY	8
LOVEABLENESS	100
ABILITY TO CHOP LOGS	110
DAD JOKE EXPERTISE	17
LEADERSHIP SKILLS (AIRPORT DAD MODE ACTIVATION)	89
FASHION FORWARDNESS	14

SPECIAL POWER?
Trained in jiu-jitsu, wushu, boxing, Krav Maga, karate and judo

You attempt to stifle your sigh of relief as the waitress arrives at your restaurant table with the bill. 'Whenever you're ready,' she says, and you wonder if you're imagining the look of sympathy she throws your way. You glance at the man across the table, who has a large smear of cheesecake still perched on his chin. He had reached across to scoop some dessert off your plate before you'd even had the chance to say whether you had, in fact, finished. But it's as he nods expectantly when you do the 'polite reach' for your purse that you know the night is a true bust. Not that you'd want to be indebted to this bland human anyway. At least the Michelin-starred food was just about worth the choke-inducing £75.11 your blind date carefully informs you is your half of the bill. He'd been the one to insist on the venue.

Last time I trust my mother to set me up on a date.

You swiftly make an excuse about heading to the loo on the way out to avoid any awkward goodbyes and jut out a hand when he seems to be leaning in for a musty hug. *Nope!* As you touch up your make-up unnecessarily, you can nevertheless say that you've absolutely slayed the outfit this evening. Shame it was all for nought . . .

Sashaying to the front of the restaurant, you head out into the warm summer air and look down at the taxi app on your phone only to see a distinct lack of cabs, so you dial your bestie to debrief on the disaster date.

' . . . and to top it off, my bank account is now looking more drained than the Sahara Desert. I can't justify a black cab, and these shoes are saying "A hike to public transport? I don't think so, sweetie!!"'

You pause as you hear a slight chuckle coming from a short distance away, on the side street where the chic restaurant is nestled. The chuckle sounds oddly familiar somehow, but –

Wait. No. No way. It can't possibly be.

A tall, slender figure clad entirely in various faded shades of black – jeans, boots, T-shirt, worn blazer – is staring down at a motorcycle, shaking his head and pushing his hair back from his face. It's long and shines darkly. In the faint, warm light shining from the restaurant windows you can see that it's streaked enticingly with just the faintest hint of grey, just like his immensely strokeable beard.

'Oh. My. Gosh,' you say into your phone, voice dropping to a murmur. 'Babe . . . I'll call you back, OK?' You absentmindedly hang up while your friend is still saying goodbye.

The man beside you turns and give an affable shrug, as though you and he are just two normal people sharing a totally normal interaction, as though it's escaped his attention that he is *Keanu Reeves.*

You'd heard he was shooting a film in London, but what are the odds that he would be here, now in front of you?

'Transport woes?' he enquires, in that oh-so-familiar raspy surfer-Canadian accent. 'Yeah, me too,' he says before you can muster an answer. He nods with an adorable head bob, then points to the motorcycle. 'A rental.' Then, in a soft voice that would definitely have coaxed you to do whatever he wanted, he adds, 'Lemme try her again.'

You clear your throat. 'It's probably the . . . ' You gesture vaguely, then smile. 'Well, I'd help you out but I've never even been on one of those things.'

He watches you for a fraction too long, and chuckles again. Then you're rendered speechless as he swings one long, jeans-clad leg over the vehicle to straddle it.

He switches the ignition, revs it, and then swings back to face you with an epic grin.

'I've been trying to get this thing going for ten minutes, and just when I might have found someone interesting to talk to, she decides to start. Maybe she's jealous.'

Is he flirting with me? 'Were you eating alone?' you somehow manage to ask.

'Post-shoot dinner.' He raises an eyebrow conspiratorially. 'I was hoping for a sneaky escape.'

'Me too. Well, not the filming part. I was—' You run to a halt. 'Sorry, I can't help but notice you're *Keanu Reeves*.'

He lets a short laugh ring up to the sky. 'Guilty,' he replies with a shrug, still grinning. You break into a sweat, fighting the urge tell him that you've been obsessed with him ever since a lax English teacher showed your class the film of *Much Ado About Nothing* and you witnessed the majesty of Keanu Charles Reeves dressed in leather.

The motorcycle still rumbles beneath him. He looks at you with one of those adorably quizzical glances you've seen over and again his movies. 'I feel like it would be ungentlemanly of me not to offer you a ride somewhere?' He nods to your phone. 'What with the cab situation and those . . . frankly *incredible* shoes.'

You restrain your jaw from falling open, and instead smile back, smoothing a hand over your outfit and looking down at your feet. 'Oh, these?' You flick your eyes up to his, hardly believing you're really flirting with Keanu actual Reeves. 'But can I trust you? "Some Cupid kills with arrows, some with traps", right?'

Keanu rears back exaggeratedly, the engine still humming between his thighs. 'Did you just quote Shakespeare at me?'

You shrug. *I knew those ten thousand viewings would pay off.*

'Well,' Keanu says, '"I would my horse had the speed of your tongue".' He gestures to the motorbike, then looks a little flushed, bashful even. You feel flushed at all this mention of tongues. But before the moment slips away from you both, you stride over to him. He reaches into a compartment at the back of the bike and hands you a helmet, before pulling on his own.

'Where to?' he asks. 'You'll have to direct me though. I'm not from these parts.'

You chuckle. 'No worries. I know a pretty cute bar near here. We could chat about the Bard.'

'Sounds good. Hop on. Careful of those shoes.' You reach out a hand to his shoulder to steady you, and feel a muscle ripple beneath the worn blazer. 'Best to keep a firm grip,' he murmurs.

Straddling the bike behind him, you take a deep breath to inhale his warm, spicy musk as you wrap your arms around his middle. Your heart rate goes into overdrive.

Is this really happening?

Just then, you both look up as you hear a photographer calling Keanu's name. He revs the engine, and you grip him tighter as he pulls away, your laughter mingling together in the night air.

Mark Ruffalo

Mark Ruffalo is a quintessential Daddy, made all the more attractive by how much he adores his wife. (Men who put their women on pedestals get an A+.) He is an American actor and producer who is most recognisable for his role as Bruce Banner/Hulk in the Marvel Cinematic Universe. His talent goes beyond this and, in fact, he is one of few performers to receive all four EGOT nominations. He's achieved all this *and* he is neurodivergent and grew up with undiagnosed dyslexia and ADHD. I'm going to put it out there, I think Mark Ruffalo might be a boss bitch.

Mark is famously incredibly forthright in both politics and in his activism. He is anti-fracking and a big supporter of environmental protection. He is anti-war, pro-choice and supports the LGBTQ+ community. I don't like to hold men up in reverence for being the most basic level of good human being but, really, they are hard to come by these days. If more men were like Mark, well, maybe we'd have some chance at equity.

'I think of marriage as a garden. You have to tend to it. Respect it, take care of it, feed it. Make sure everyone is getting the right amount of . . . sunlight.'

DADDY SCORE

Mark Ruffalo

OVERALL DADDY/ZADDY SCORE	62
ATTAINABILITY	-50
LOVEABLENESS	98
ABILITY TO CHOP LOGS	46
DAD JOKE EXPERTISE	32
LEADERSHIP SKILLS (AIRPORT DAD MODE ACTIVATION)	89
FASHION FORWARDNESS	21

SPECIAL POWER?
Climate activist

Jeff Goldblum

The eclectic and the vibrant Jeff Goldblum has reached almost mythical levels of Daddy. Born to a Russian-Jewish father and an Austrian-Jewish mother, Jeffrey Lynn Goldblum was born and raised in Pittsburgh, Pennsylvania, famous for its number of bridges (it has 446) and of course, for giving the world Jeff.

Jeff began his career on the stage in New York and with his unique voice and delivery, he quickly made an impression. In fact, he was so impactful, a single line he delivered in Woody Allen's *Annie Hall* (1977) stood out to moviegoers. Our quirky king made his quirky name in films such as *The Adventures of Buckaroo Banzai Across the 8th Dimension* (1984), *Into the Night* (1985) and the remake of *The Fly* (1986) which really was his breakthrough moment on screen.

Since then, Jeff Goldblum has starred in some of the highest-grossing films such as *Jurassic Park* (1993) and *Independence Day* (1996). Soon he will be starring in the upcoming film *Wicked* as the Wonderful Wizard of Oz and I simply cannot *wait* for that.

On top of this, he is also an accomplished jazz pianist (hot!).

'Life finds a way.'

DADDY SCORE

Jeff Goldblum

OVERALL DADDY/ZADDY SCORE	102
ATTAINABILITY	-10
LOVEABLENESS	100
ABILITY TO CHOP LOGS	42
DAD JOKE EXPERTISE	85
LEADERSHIP SKILLS (AIRPORT DAD MODE ACTIVATION)	25
FASHION FORWARDNESS	77

SPECIAL POWER?
Jazz piano

Robert Downey Jr.

I'd describe Robert Downey Jr. as the bad boy of the acting world. He exudes a mildly toxic energy that I'm afraid to say, is highly attractive. (I never said women were sane with their desires!)

One of the most revered and respected actors in Hollywood, Robert Downey Jr.'s life has had ups and downs that would make Shakespeare don his ruff and pick up his pen. Born in Manhattan, New York, to a director and filmographer father and an actress mother, it would seem Robert was destined to be in this world and he was immersed in drama and theatre from a very young age. In fact, he made his acting debut at the age of five years old in his father's film *Pound*.

Throughout the eighties and nineties, Robert built up his film repertoire and in 1992 he received a nomination for an Academy Award and won the BAFTA for his performance in the title role of *Chaplin*.

In the late nineties he was starring in films alongside names such as Ian McKellen, Hugh Grant, Woody Harrelson, Juliette Lewis, Sean Penn, Patrick Dempsey, Ben Stiller and Claudia Schiffer. In 2001, he made his primetime television debut as attorney Larry Paul in *Ally McBeal* and for this he won a Golden Globe and a Screen Actors Guild Award and was nominated for an Emmy.

It was also during the late nineties that his drug-related problems escalated, resulting in arrests and leading to him staying in a court-ordered drug treatment programme. Following treatment, he has maintained his sobriety since 2003.

He worked hard to rebuild his career, and took some time to foray into music too – he has an incredible singing voice alongside all his other talents!

He set the world alight in his starring role as Ironman in the Marvel films, and has made a name for himself across the action, drama *and* comedy genres. Some of his best films being in the latter space such as *Due Date*.

Robert has a wife (sigh), and three kids, who he adores. Downey also serves on the board of the Anti-Recidivism Coalition that advocates for criminal justice reform and recently changed his diet to veganism to reduce his carbon footprint and make a positive change to help the environment. We love a man who supports good causes!

'Worrying is like praying for something you don't want to happen.'

DADDY SCORE

Robert Downey Jr.

OVERALL DADDY/ZADDY SCORE	95
ATTAINABILITY	0
LOVEABLENESS	20
ABILITY TO CHOP LOGS	75
DAD JOKE EXPERTISE	90
LEADERSHIP SKILLS (AIRPORT DAD MODE ACTIVATION) (He literally helped lead the Avengers)	99
FASHION FORWARDNESS	80

SPECIAL POWER?
Bad boy supreme

When Beyoncé said 'Renaissance yachting in Capri,' you took her words as gospel and hopped on a plane to the Amalfi coast. Now, this is the land of the rich and famous. Wealth is in the air, and it smells like the finest fragrance money can buy.

As you walk through the streets of Capri, surrounded by millionaires, billionaires and multi-multi-squillionaires you are folded into this unbelievable world where bank balances are as long as phone numbers. You pass Prada, Bottega, Gucci, Chanel and Louis Vuitton and it feels like the sensory overwhelm the upper classes must have felt when they stumbled across East London back in the oompah-pah days. The best part of it all though, is that even with all of the designers, colours and money people competing and vying for attention it is *you* who stands out. Eyes catch yours as you smile knowingly to yourself.

You take a seat in a café bar outside a hotel, where other people – tourists, locals and of course, regulars – are also enjoying some shade. You order yourself a coffee, '*Per favore posso avere un caffè, signore,*' and sip on the rich Italian espresso, surveying the morning bustle that unfolds before you.

As you are relaxing into this world, you are completely unaware of a man looking at you, a few tables along. He has thick-rimmed sunglasses that hide eyes that are full of mischief. He wears a smart shirt and trousers, everything clean and ironed to perfection, the heat seemingly having no impact on him at all. The watch on his wrist is the only thing that betrays this man's wealth. He sips on his coffee, stealing glances at you.

In your oblivious state, you don't notice the same man paying your bill and sending you over a mimosa. The waiter approaches you and tells you a gentleman has paid for everything and sent you this drink. Your eyebrows jump up in surprise. 'È giusto?' *Is that right?* You ask. You glance over at the man the waiter has gestured to and smile. You hope your warmth doesn't betray the intense excitement you feel at seeing this man for the first time, the handsome face unmistakeably belonging to one of the most famous actors in the world.

As you sip the fizzing mango mimosa, the man has decided to make his move. The effortless confidence that could easily breach into arrogance is obvious in each step. He gestures to the chair next to you.

'May I?'

You nod, obligingly, before your eyes return to the comers and goers of the pristine Capri streets.

He sits quietly. Shocked by your nonchalance.

'I've never seen you here before,' he says.

'That's because I've never been here before,' you reply.

'Well, I'm glad you decided to visit today.'

You don't betray the anticipation that is enveloping you, but you turn to him more explicitly, 'So why did you send me this drink?' You sip the mimosa and sustain eye contact with him.

'I wanted to know who you are. And you looked like a woman who should be drinking a mimosa. I don't suppose you could tell me your name?'

You tell him. He smiles. 'I'm Robert.'

'A pleasure.'

You look at each other in a way that is totally uninhibited and full of desire. You knew who he was as soon as you laid eyes on him. Robert Downey Jr.

He seems to enjoy your recognition.

'I wonder if I could tempt you to join me for more drinks. We could go to my yacht?'

You almost choke on your mimosa. *His yacht*.

He notices your energy at the suggestion. 'I'm just moored up in the harbour. I'll tell you something, it's an entirely different experience seeing Capri from a private yacht.'

A smirk crosses your lips. 'And how do I know you won't kidnap me?'

For the first time, Robert laughs. He seems a lot more welcoming when he does so. His teeth are so perfectly straight and white. The laughter creates an ease that had been missing in the dance of your first interaction.

He places a hand to his chest. 'I solemnly swear I will not kidnap you.'

You chuckle, 'I guess there are worse ways to be kidnapped than on a yacht in Capri. In fact, what am I saying? Please *do* kidnap me.'

'As you wish.' He stands and puts his hand on the back of your chair beckoning you to join him.

You stand, and once again, eyes are on you, but now they are on both of you. The rich celebrity, and the mysterious woman he seems to be completely taken with.

You move together back through the streets that had had you in complete awe not so long ago, and now you feel like you could truly belong there.

Robert holds his arm out and you take it, feeling his bicep tensed against the fine material of his shirt. As you walk, he leans closer to whisper in your ear, 'I would buy you any of this. Anything you wanted.'

Your heart thumps in your chest.

Later, you lay back on a sunlounger, the sun fading towards the horizon and the sky filled with a more subtle orange and red hue. As you relax, Robert approaches, and passes you another mimosa. There have been mimosas in your hand pretty much all day. He sits beside you and picks up your other hand, kissing it, his stubble grazing your skin and filling you with hot liquid yearning.

'You were right,' you say, eyes locked to his, knowing the passion the setting of the sun will bring.

'How is that?' He looks back with equal intensity, his eyes feasting on your lips with a hunger.

'Capri is a different experience on a private yacht.'

He takes your glass puts it aside and pulls you to him, a strong firm hand against your cheek. You kiss deeply, drinking each other in. The richness of life outshining any grand wealth this island might store.

Denzel Washington

Denzel Hayes Washington Jr. Phew! What a legend. It feels slightly wrong to be listing him here: he should be esteemed as a king, not a Daddy. Too late now, though. Denzel started his life in Mount Vernon, New York, and no one expected him to rise to the levels of fame and acclaim he has today. His accolades are numerous. He is, at time of writing, the recipient of a Tony Award, two Academy Awards, three Golden Globe Awards, two Silver Bears, the Cecil B DeMille Lifetime Achievement Award and the Presidential Medal of Freedom. The *New York Times* named him the greatest actor of the twenty-first century.

How does he do it? With real graft! Starting out on off-Broadway shows, he built up versatility to secure his first big screen roles in *Carbon Copy* (1981). Following his Oscar win in 1989 for his role in *Glory* came stand-out performances in *Malcolm X*, *Training Day*, *Man on Fire*, *Flight*, *The Equalizer*, *American Gangster* and *Fences*.

A philanthropist and advocate, he is the spokesperson for the Boys & Girls Clubs of America and contributes to charities like the Nelson Mandela Children's Fund.

'If you don't fail, you're not even trying.'

Denzel Washington

OVERALL DADDY/ZADDY SCORE   10
(to be respectful)

ATTAINABILITY   0

LOVEABLENESS   100

ABILITY TO CHOP LOGS   95

DAD JOKE EXPERTISE   20

LEADERSHIP SKILLS   99
(AIRPORT DAD MODE ACTIVATION)

FASHION FORWARDNESS   51

SPECIAL POWER?
Authority and leadership skills

Ryan Gosling

I'm a Barbie girl and he's . . . just Ken.

Could there be anything more endearing than a silly billy dorky himbo with golden retriever energy? Ryan Gosling is boyfriend *and* goofy dad coded, and more than deserving of the Daddy title.

Ryan is the French-Canadian son of a secretary and travelling salesman andexcelled in drama and fine arts at school. He is one of the stars who was picked for The Mickey Mouse Club in the nineties, alongside stars such as Justin Timberlake, Britney Spears and Christina Aguilera. Though he had no formal acting training he quickly launched his acting career appearing in series and films. It was his role in *The Believer* (2001) that really attracted attention, though, and he was nominated for an Independent Spirit Award and the Golden Aries award.

We know him today as the ultimate romantic drama and comedy lead, breaking the hearts of more women than potentially any other man in the world in his role as Noah in *The Notebook* (2004). And that chemistry between him and co-star Rachel McAdams felt real because it was very real – the pair dated for three years following the film.

His performances in *Crazy, Stupid, Love* (2011) and *La La Land* (2016), both opposite actress Emma Stone (lucky woman), demonstrated he really is the jewel in the film romance crown.

And he has been awarded for his valiant efforts to make the world fall in love with him as the recipient of a Golden Globe and two Academy Award nominations. He is the people's Ken and who knows, maybe another Academy Award nomination might be coming his way for that performance of the decade.

Now, he is horrifically and heartbreakingly passionately in love with his wife, who is none other than *the* Eva Mendes. Together they have two children and a Doberman and I'm sure live in perpetual domestic blisss. Good for them I guess.

'I'm just sort of making it up as I go along.'

DADDY SCORE

Ryan Gosling

OVERALL DADDY/ZADDY SCORE	100
ATTAINABILITY	0
LOVEABLENESS	101
ABILITY TO CHOP LOGS (he was even a lumber mill worker in *The Notebook*)	99
DAD JOKE EXPERTISE	97
LEADERSHIP SKILLS (AIRPORT DAD MODE ACTIVATION) (*'What do you want?'*)	95
FASHION FORWARDNESS	93
SPECIAL POWER? Our favourite himbo!	

I t's your first day on set. This is a moment you have been working up to for a long time.

The romantic lead roles are difficult to land and even harder to pull off, but you are up for the challenge.

You sip your green tea as you look over the script for the scenes of the day while the hairdresser works their magic. Your agent sits across from you, tapping away at her laptop.

'Are you nervous?'

You swallow. 'A bit.'

She nods. 'I've heard he's one of the loveliest people in the business to work with. And as he's been in the industry a bit longer, hopefully he can make you feel at ease during your scenes.'

You look at yourself in the mirror. Your hair swept back into an elegant ponytail, your eye make-up natural and the blush pulling a warmth into your cheeks and echoing the colour on your lips. You check your teeth for the five hundredth time and take deep breaths.

'I hope so.'

When the time arrives to commence the scene, your heart feels like it's moved up your trachea and lodged itself in your throat for the foreseeable. The butterflies swarm in your stomach and even as the director smiles welcomingly at you, you wonder what the hell you are doing here.

Then you hear a voice behind you.

'How you doing?' You know exactly who it is because you've been watching him since you were a teen. Lying on your stomach in front of the TV screen, hands cupped under your chin, heart thumping as he launches into his monologue, 'What do you *want*?' he implores

Rachel McAdams, and you sigh. To be loved like that. To be so determinedly and unfathomably insistent on making something work when everything is telling you it shouldn't.

The memory is playing in your head as you turn around and your eyes land upon him, Ryan Gosling. He's just as handsome in real life, if not more so. The smile lines marked into his face enhance his charisma and the sparkle in his eyes is not something that could be sufficiently captured by pixels.

You don't betray any of the nerves that pulse under your skin, this is your time and you know that Ryan Gosling is just as aware of you as you are of him. 'Hi!' You reach out your hand to shake his. 'I'm doing good . . . I think? I mean this is all surreal but I'm excited. Ready to get started.'

Ryan puts his hands in his pockets after your handshake and nods. 'I've seen your recent work. You're good. I've been really looking forward to shooting with you.'

The gasp you gusp and the gulp you galp could surely have been heard from somewhere far beyond these set walls. Maybe in Timbuktu? That's the place people tend to refer to when they want to suggest somewhere faraway.

You both catch eyes and are quiet for a moment before he starts laughing. 'You held on to the professionalism for a solid thirty seconds there, impressive.'

'I am actually entirely unphased by one of my favourite romantic lead actors telling me I am also a good actress. In fact, it happens to me almost every week. It was Matthew McConaughey the other day.'

Ryan rubs his chin, 'I don't know whether to be honoured or offended by that.'

You groan. 'I was trying to be cavalier. I'm a huge fan, if you hadn't guessed. God, that's embarrassing.'

'It's endearing.'

'It's unhinged.'

'Unhinged *and* endearing.'

'Hey, I'm pretty sure that's what the director asked me to convey in this character.'

'Oh, so you're method acting.'

'I think that's less awkward than saying this is just me?'

'Method acting it is.' He nods, his eyes seem like they are seeking to delve deeper, to know you further, but in that moment, he is called away to hair and make-up. 'Well, it was lovely to meet you, and I'm looking forward to seeing how much more unhinged you become as we continue working on this film together.'

You swear to yourself as he walks away. *Of course, I would come out with some rubbish like that and manage to half offend one of the finest looking men on God's earth.*

The other half of your brain is preparing for the scene you are doing together later that day. *At least it won't be hard to pretend you fancy him.*

As the day continues and you get settled into your performance, you feel more at ease and the butterflies have evaporated. You know you are delivering and impressing because the director is giving all the signs that they are happy, and even excited, about the scenes you are doing. Once or twice, you look out beyond the set at cast and crew trying to spot him but you can't see him. *He's probably giving me a wide berth*, you think. *I don't blame him.*

But then you look up once more in-between takes and you spot him. With his hands stuffed in his pockets and his demeanour calm, he looks at you with his eyebrows slightly raised, as if surprised by you in some way. He quickly turns away when you catch his eye and you feel confused, hoping he isn't regretting starring in this film with you.

When your scene together arrives, he walks up to you and grins cheekily.

'I have something to confess.'

You are taken aback, 'OK?'

'I'm really the unhinged one out of us both.'

You chuckle, 'How's that?'

'Because I have been waiting all day to do this scene with you, impatiently, because I really, *really* want to kiss you.'

You are floored and your face must show extreme shock because Ryan quickly follows up, 'God, I'm sorry. That's so unprofessional. This never happens.' He looks downcast and his cheeks blaze with embarrassment.

His eyes are on the floor when you take his arm. 'That makes two of us.'

Looking back at you, his mouth widens into that Hollywood smile that had electrified you through the screen. It has the power to knock you out in person.

'I think we're going to make this film pretty convincing.'

You revel in the secret knowledge shared between you.

'I think so too.'

The bustle to get ready for the scene continues around you, but you feel like it's only you and Ryan in the world. And when the director says 'Lights. Camera. Action,' both of you know there will be no acting required.

Usher
Raymond IV

Usher might not seem like a typical Daddy candidate, but at the age of forty-four and as the father of R&B as well as four children, he is a strong contender. There's something distinctly seductive about your name featuring roman numerals and I won't be explaining that any further.

Usher was born in Dallas, Texas and was just 12 when was scouted at a singing competition. His second album *My Way* (1997) skyrocketed Usher into fame and since then he has become an icon, selling more than eighty million records worldwide, making him one of the best-selling music artists of all time.

Usher's songs are some of the sexiest in the world and 'Nice & Slow' alone is likely the reason for a good number of pregnancies in the last 25 years. Much more than his sex appeal, Usher is also a philanthropist, founding a charity to provide young people with a new look on life through education and experience.

Usher's Tiny Desk, an intimate live performance streamed on YouTube, electrified his fans and commenced his Daddy era.

'The best present a man can give a woman is his undivided attention.'

DADDY SCORE

Usher Raymond TV

OVERALL DADDY/ZADDY SCORE	92
ATTAINABILITY	95
LOVEABLENESS	74
ABILITY TO CHOP LOGS	44
DAD JOKE EXPERTISE	12
LEADERSHIP SKILLS (AIRPORT DAD MODE ACTIVATION)	88
FASHION FORWARDNESS	99

SPECIAL POWER?
Music

he lights dim, and there is a red hue that covers the stage. The set is sultry and sexy, and you gasp as you hear the opening to the song that may as well have invented romance.

Usher opens his show with 'Superstar', and your body tingles as he croons 'This is for you, you, my number one.' This has been the moment you've waited for for a long time. Usher had been the soundtrack to your teenage years, the glint in his eye and the smooth moves of his body forming a crush that had taken hold and never let go with the passing of the years. When he walks out on stage in front of you and the intimate audience that have been lucky enough to get tickets, the cacophony of applause and cheers fills your head and you join in, dancing to the songs you love the most in the world.

Usher moves like water. Each step flows into the next and you can tell it comes as easy to him as breathing, as blinking. His voice is like smooth aged whiskey and thick honey, blessing every eardrum in the room. You are just another person in the crowds of people who cheer his name, but during the chorus for 'Nice & Slow' you think he looks at you. His eyebrow raises slightly. His smile widens, almost imperceptibly. But you know it's for you, you're not like other girls. The thrill lifts you and you swing your hips to the beat, your friends around you bursting at the seams with joy, backing you and celebrating you as all attention in the room diverts to you for a few moments of the show.

As the performance comes to an end and the encore draws to a close, you feel completely overwhelmed with satisfaction. The night had been everything you wanted it to be and more. You turn to leave with your girls, ready for the end of the night and maybe some chicken nuggets to finish off, when someone taps you on the shoulder. You turn, expecting to have left something behind, and realise it's one of the crew.

'Please can you come with me? Usher would like to meet you.'

Your mouth gapes open and your friends are gagged, their eyes switching between each other and the man who surely *must* be having you on.

'Err, OK?'

'Your friends can come too. It's this way.'

You follow the man towards the back of the stage and you feel like you are hallucinating or levitating as you see the sign BACKSTAGE on a big black door ahead and you pass through in stunned silence.

Through the doors is a lounge area where Usher's entourage mill around, drinking, partying and celebrating the end of a show perfectly executed. They look to you and your friends and smile warmly, knowingly, and pass you drinks of strong liquor. The member of the crew who approached you initially beckons you specifically, and you move to follow him a bit further on, leaving your girls to get to know Usher's team.

You move into a dressing room and there across the room, sat on the sofa sipping his drink, is Usher. *The* Usher. And he looks at you with a gaze that is so piercing, so exposing, that you feel you might drop to the floor in shock.

'Thanks Jay. Hey, I was hoping you would come. Come sit.' Usher gestures to the sofa, and you walk across in a way you pray looks effortless and sexy.

'H-hi.'

He laughs. A laugh that is cool, calm, collected, but also one that can't help but make people around feel at ease, and immediately the tension disappears from your shoulders. 'I realise this is a bit intense but . . . I saw you in the crowd and I felt drawn to you. I just thought maybe we could hang out, or I could get to know you a bit better?'

You lock eyes with him, and you sit like that for a minute. Appraising each other. Enjoying each other. You can't believe you have gone from singing this man's songs in your bedroom to being sat opposite him in his dressing room. Real life really is stranger than fiction.

You cough, scared your voice might not work ever again, before saying, 'I'd be up for that. You know, it's funny, I thought you were looking at me during the show, but I just figured I'd made it up.'

He groans, 'Did I make it that obvious? Man, I thought I was smooth.'

A confidence takes hold of you and you nudge him gently, 'No it was very subtle. A skill perfected over time, no?'

Usher shakes his head. 'I actually haven't done this before. Like, honestly. People tend to come to me. That sounds so braggy or whatever but yeah. I just thought you looked dope and there was something about your smile, it just spoke to me.' He rubs his chin and shifts closer to you. Did he look *nervous*?

'Is that right?' You lean your leg against his, and you can feel his warmth and all of your starstruck buzzing energy seems to evaporate. He's just a guy, you're just a girl, and you're here together. That's it.

He licks his lower lip in that way that men do that is so painfully and horrifically sexy. 'You stood out. You *stand* out.'

You look at his lips, full and plump, and back up to his eyes, bright and mischievous. You know this is a risk, and you know it could all be a farce, but in that moment you really, *really* don't care. What did Usher sing? *I'll be your groupie baby.* She couldn't tell if it was him or her who was the superstar because in that dressing room, the spotlight was on them both, and they shone together.

Usher reaches up to your chin and with the same mouth that has sung all your favourite hits, and delivered your most adored lyrics, he kisses you.

And you barely stop till the next show.

Will Smith

Will Smith was one of my first crushes. That backwards cap used to make my heart go pitter patter. The original cheeky guy, Willard Carroll Smith II is an American actor, comedian, producer, rapper and songwriter who has enjoyed success across film, television and music. He has been recognised an Academy Award, BAFTA and four Grammy awards, as well as being nominated for five Golden Globes and two more Academy Awards.

Since playing a fictionalised version of himself in *The Fresh Prince of Bel-Air*, he has become one of the most recognisable faces in the film industry, starring in classic films such as *Bad Boys* (1995), *Men in Black* (1997), *Ali* (2001), *I, Robot* (2004), *Hitch* (2005), *The Pursuit of Happyness* (2006), *I Am Legend* (2007) and *Seven Pounds* (2008), to name just a few. He is ranked as the most bankable star worldwide by Forbes, and the films in which he has had leading roles have accumulated worldwide gross earnings of over $100 million each. Hard-working and machine-like in his drive to achieve, Will has overcome public backlash as well as racism and prejudice in the industry to remain a legend of epic proportions.

'Money and success don't change people; they merely amplify what's already there.'

DADDY SCORE

Will Smith

OVERALL DADDY/ZADDY SCORE	95
ATTAINABILITY	35
LOVEABLENESS	52
ABILITY TO CHOP LOGS	100
DAD JOKE EXPERTISE	95
LEADERSHIP SKILLS (AIRPORT DAD MODE ACTIVATION)	100
FASHION FORWARDNESS	88

SPECIAL POWER?
That scene in *I, Robot* where he does pull-ups

'I feel like we need to discuss that scene in I, Robot where Will Smith is doing pull-ups topless. It just feels like an important, life-altering event that really deserves attention in this busy modern world.'

Tweet

Y ou press 'post' on the tweet as you relax back into your sofa, your third glass of Provence rosé heating your cheeks and intoxicating your mind. You know your tweets are the most unhinged in these moments when you're deliciously tipsy, and it feels satisfying to release something so silly into the ether, for people to see your words and maybe laugh, possibly ignore them, either way, it doesn't really matter. It's your profile. You can say what you like, and this evening you fancy leaning into your thirst.

You press play on *I, Robot* again, rewinding to the scene you refer to in the tweet.

Wow. That is a man. You think.

As the film continues playing, you continue sipping and the wine makes you impatient for a thrill. And what do we do when we fancy a hit of endorphins? We scroll on our phones.

You open up Twitter, seeing the sixty-eight likes that have amassed on the tweet. The girlies replying, 'and I oop', 'let's talk about it!' and 'that's a world-shifting event of note, that's for sure'. You giggle at your community, all equally revelling in the silliness.

You continue scrolling for a little while, eyes glazed, and then you notice a notification for a DM pop up. You expect it to be your friend sending you some hilarious tweet or meme that closely relates to you because really, we all live the same lives.

Sitting up like you've just been electrocuted, some of your wine spills over onto your hand and your leg. You put the glass down quickly, wipe off the liquid and look back at your phone in complete and utter disbelief. There, in your DMs, is @WillSmith – the real and blue tick verified Will Smith – with a message written directly to you.

You put a hand over your mouth. *What in the actual hell*? You know you tagged him but *seriously* it's Will Smith?! When does he ever look at Twitter? Your anxiety builds until you can't take it anymore and you have to open the DM. He has forwarded you the tweet and made a comment.

@WillSmith: Let's discuss it. I'm interested to hear your thoughts.

Surely there is no possible way that this is the real Will Smith. That is crazy.

You shake your head and reply, convinced this is some kind of farce.

@BaddieBabe: Happy to discuss it with the real Will Smith any time.

He replies straight away.

@WillSmith: What makes you think this isn't me?

@BaddieBabe: Life? Science? Reality? All of the above?

@WillSmith: Cool. Let me rectify that.

@WillSmith sent a photo

Now, your hand shakes. Either you are going to be rick rolled or embarrassed by some random person controlling Will's account, or this is a legitimate message from the superstar himself.

You open the photo and look for a moment before flinging your phone to the other side of the sofa bursting out with a scream, cackle and gasp all at once. *No flippin way!* You pick the phone up again gently like it's a poisonous animal and look closer at the photo. *You have got to be kidding me.*

It's him, there's no question about it. And it's him pointing at the tweet you just sent, with his phone date and time reading today's date and the time from a few minutes ago.

You get another message through.

@WillSmith: You convinced now?

You breathe through your nose and out through your mouth. You try to unmuddle your thoughts that feel stuck in the foggy clouds of your tipsy mind. You sit back, and look up at the younger Will Smith whose face is on your TV screen, then you look back at the older, mature Will Smith who has just sent his photo. Everything feels completely incongruous and surreal. *But sod it,* you think, *why not lean into it?*

@WillSmith: Hello?

@BaddieBabe: Well, looks like we should have the conversation.

@WillSmith: So tell me, what was so life-altering about that particular scene for you?

@BaddieBabe: I think seeing this man hardened to vulnerability, using physical exercise to channel a hidden conflict was a particularly powerful expression of character, and the intense masculinity of the scene had a profound effect on me.

@BaddieBabe: Oh, and you looked fit.

@WillSmith: I see.

Your stomach constricts. *I've given it away too quickly.* This game of flirtation that is played, this back and forth, the give and receive, is always risky. Sometimes too much straight away sends everything off kilter.

You see Will typing.

@WillSmith: I feel like I need to hear more of your deep thoughts and considerations. And I equally have some of my own. Maybe we could come together and discuss further?

Heat travels up your body and passion tingles up your inner thighs. This same man is the one you have fancied for half of your life. *Surely he can't be suggesting he would come and see me?!*

@BaddieBabe: I always have plenty to say but it might be hard, I'm in London and I'm guessing you're in LA?

@WillSmith: I'll come.

He'll come?

@WillSmith: What do you say, tomorrow at the Marriott Hotel Bar? 8pm?

You squeal. Your neighbours are probably cursing you in the above and below flats. You know this could be a complete sham, and you might turn up tomorrow and he won't be there. It could be a non-starter. But it could also be one *hell* of a story. One for the memoir, if ever there was one.

And so, despite all your sensible instincts telling you to get in line, you let the risk-taking thoughts win and you type back:

@BaddieBabe: I'll see you there.

Dwayne Johnson

You know you have to be a certain calibre of man to be known by everyone as 'The Rock'. No doubt most of us would like to climb that mountain ourselves.

The son of a professional wrestler with Black and Samoan heritage, he was almost drafted into the NFL. After suffering a back injury, he decided to commit to wrestling and made his debut under the name Flex Kavana. He joined the WWE and became a key member of 'The Nation of Domination' group (hot) and took on the persona of The Rock. He rose to global prominence, aided by the gimmick he had as a charismatic trash talker. He is a ten-time world champion, including the first of African-American descent.

After his first role in *The Mummy Returns* (2001), he took over the action/family film space with *The Scorpion King* (2002), *Jumanji: Welcome to the Jungle* (2017), *G.I. Joe: Retaliation* (2013), the *Fast & Furious* film series (2011-2023), and *Moana (2016)*. He owns his own production company and is the founder of a charity working with at-risk and terminally ill children.

'Success isn't always about greatness. It's about consistency. Consistent hard work leads to success. Greatness will come.'

DADDY SCORE

Dwayne Johnson

OVERALL DADDY/ZADDY SCORE	110
ATTAINABILITY	0
LOVEABLENESS	100
ABILITY TO CHOP LOGS	110
DAD JOKE EXPERTISE	98
LEADERSHIP SKILLS (AIRPORT DAD MODE ACTIVATION)	100
FASHION FORWARDNESS	82

SPECIAL POWER?
Could carry you anywhere

ONE, TWO, THREE, FOUR . . .
. . . NINE, TEN, ELEVEN AND TWELVE!

You exhale loudly as you place the barbell back on the rack. Your quads are shaking so you stretch up and then push back into a squat, holding the position. It has been a quiet evening at the gym, and you've been focused, pushing towards your goals and enjoying the main character energy of being one of the only people there. You stand up and roll your shoulders back and take a minute to check yourself out in the mirror. Mmmhmm, the matching set you're wearing is making everything look particularly good. Gym sets really have the power to transform your self-esteem in half a millisecond.

Back at the squat rack, you're determined to up your weight and decide to be a bit extra with it today. If you squat this, it would be your personal best. You press play on the music that gets you particularly hyped up and launch into the squat.

ONE. You say under your breath.

TWO. That's exactly it! You're strong as hell!

THREE! Oh *shit*.

Your legs wobble beneath you and you try to push up but no matter what you do, your muscles aren't responding. You believe it's over, you're about to fall to the ground in a heap when you suddenly feel the weight become light again. What is this? Some divine intervention? You rise like the weight is nothing and then it really is nothing, because it is no longer on your shoulders. Instead it is gripped in the hand – please note the singular hand – of the huge man who is stood behind you.

'Woah, I thought that was over for you then.' He places the weight on the rack like it was a feather rather than your own personal best.

You take a moment to consider your legs, but thankfully they are still fully functioning. 'Tell me about it. Thought I was a goner.'

You finally take a proper look at your rescuer, and your heart almost drops out of your butt.

There, towering over you, taking up an obscene amount of space, is The Rock, looking as sturdy, hard and immoveable as his namesake. Before you can help it your mouth gapes open. *There is no way I've just been saved from a gym calamity by Dwayne 'The Rock' Johnson.*

He looks at the weight you just lifted, 'Woah, that's some weight. Impressive.'

The Rock just said I'm impressive. 'From the way you just picked it up with your little finger, it doesn't feel like that.'

He laughs, filling the empty gym with bass. He really looks like he's been carved out of marble. He has the aura of a demi-god warrior like Hercules, Achilles… or, well, Maui incarnate. The fact he is working out in your gym is still not quite making sense.

'I've never seen you here before, you new to this gym?'

He nods, 'We're filming near here and I have an apartment in this complex. This is literally my first time here. Thought it was empty until I heard a small squeal coming from the weight racks.'

You groan. 'I squealed?!'

A grin lights up his face, 'It was sweet, really.'

In that moment, as his eyes glint at you, flirtation seeping into your conversation with ease, you are unbelievably grateful that you wore your best gym set. The energy between you is building into a heat and both of you sense it.

Dwayne coughs, 'How about we train together? I can prevent you from further travesty, and you can teach me a thing or two about hitting a squat that deep.'

Dwayne 'The Rock' Johnson wants to train with me. I'm going to fall over. Faking it till you make it, you feign confidence, 'I can *try* and teach you, but really, this kind of squatting is for people who are pretty advanced.'

That cheeky smile returns to his face and it's completely delicious. From the way he gazes at you, you can tell he's thinking something similar about you. 'Hit me with it.'

And so there you are training with The Rock for the next hour. The session is so intense you know the DOMS are going to be horrific the next day, but you don't care. The adrenaline of the moment is allowing you to hit personal best after personal best. When he assists with your chin ups, hands on your waist and hips, there is a fizzing all over your body. He lifts you like you weigh absolutely nothing at all. When he puts you down and you turn to him, the desire radiates off him. You keep it moving, not one to give into temptation that quickly. When you squat again and he supports the barbell for you, you catch him glancing at your butt which you *know* is looking particularly round and juicy. You push it out just a bit more to tease him.

By the end, you are both hot, in more ways than one. You laugh together and as you head towards the exit, he pauses at the doorway. 'That might be the best workout

I've ever done, and hell, I've done a lot.'

The way his skin glistens with sweat, and the fact that his mountainous form seems to cover you in shadow sends shockwaves through you again. You stop and look at each other.

'Can I?' he asks.

You breathe, 'Yes.'

He leans over you, a hand above your head, while one reaches around to your lower back. You're backed against the doorframe, literally between a rock and a hard place. He lifts you slightly into him and whispers, 'Same time tomorrow?' before he kisses you.

Passion sears your skin and seems to weave you together. The endorphins of the workout entwine with the endorphins of this desire and by the time you stop making out, you feel ready to do it all over again and like you could lift any weight in the world.

Henry Golding

Henry Golding is Malaysian and English and was born in Kuching, Sarawak, Malaysia. He spent his early years in Terengganu before moving to England when he was eight. At twenty-one he returned to Malaysia and pursued acting work, becoming the host of travel shows there.

Henry became globally known when he debuted on the big screen in the smash hit *Crazy Rich Asians* (2018) where he played a very hot, very rich Singaporean multi-millionaire heir. Since then he has starred in multiple things including *A Simple Favour* (2018), *Last Christmas* (2019) and *The Gentlemen* (2019).

Word on the street is that there will be two sequels to *Crazy Rich Asians* in which Henry will reprise his role as Nick Young, and we are looking forward to all the performances to come from this fairly young Daddy (at time of writing, he's thirty-six).

'I just wanna make great movies. I'm neither half white nor half Asian. I'm full both. You need to take pride in where you're from.'

DADDY SCORE

Henry Golding

OVERALL DADDY/ZADDY SCORE	62
ATTAINABILITY	0
LOVEABLENESS	89
ABILITY TO CHOP LOGS	75
DAD JOKE EXPERTISE	22
LEADERSHIP SKILLS (AIRPORT DAD MODE ACTIVATION)	34
FASHION FORWARDNESS	81

SPECIAL POWER?
Charm

Ryan Reynolds

Ryan Reynolds is a hot, wholesome Daddy with *edge*. Famously passionately in love with his beautiful wife and caring mother of his children, Blake Lively, he might be the least attainable in this whole book. But we can enjoy imagining a different reality; if Marvel can create alternative universes, so can we!

Born in Vancouver, Canada, Ryan is the youngest of four children. He was involved in acting from the age of thirteen, attaining a few small roles in TV series, but at nineteen he became discouraged and quit acting to pursue an alternative career. Thankfully, he was persuaded to try acting again by his friend and fellow actor Chris William Martin and so he moved to LA – as so many do – with big dreams and little money.

Ryan gained traction as an actor in his roles in romantic comedies and action movies throughout the early 2000s. Romantic comedy films such as *Definitely, Maybe* (2008) and *The Proposal* (2009) secured his place as the handsome and hilarious heart-throb, but it was his Marvel film *Deadpool* (2016) that garnered him worldwide fame and attention. His acting performance in *Deadpool* gained him nominations in the Critics' Choice Movie Awards and the Golden Globe Awards. Since then, he has starred in a number of action, action-comedy and animated films that have secured his name in the Hollywood hall of fame.

Notably, Ryan is also an astute businessman with multiple strings to his bow. He founded and drives his production company, Maximum Effort, has a stake in Aviation American Gin and an ownership stake in Mint Mobile, and in 2021 he purchased Wrexham AFC, a Welsh football club, with *It's Always Sunny in Philadelphia* star, Rob McElhenney. Ryan and Rob's investment in and takeover of Wrexham AFC has been documented in the series *Welcome to Wrexham*. His philanthropy is equally as impressive, with him and his wife pledging $1 million to Ukrainian refugees fleeing conflict and donating $500,000 to provide indigenous people in Canada with clean water and to train young people to become professional technicians in environmental issues.

Named *People* magazine's Sexiest Man Alive in 2010, and probably dubbed the same title by thousands of women since, it's no surprise that Ryan has dated some of the baddest bitches in town including Alanis Morrissette, Scarlett Johansson and of course, his wife, Blake Lively. To top it all off he is also a devoted father of three girls and a baby (CUTE)!

'Laughing can serve you in dark moments and even help you crawl your way back out.'

DADDY SCORE

Ryan Reynolds

OVERALL DADDY/ZADDY SCORE	88
ATTAINABILITY	-100
LOVEABLENESS	54
ABILITY TO CHOP LOGS	65
DAD JOKE EXPERTISE	92
LEADERSHIP SKILLS (AIRPORT DAD MODE ACTIVATION)	86
FASHION FORWARDNESS	46

SPECIAL POWER?
Could help you make wise investments

Javier Bardem

That's King Triton to you and me!

Javier Ángel Encinas Bardem is not only the sea king, but a king among Daddies too. The Spanish actor was born in Las Palmas in the Canary Islands and is the son of the actress Pilar Bardem. In fact, Javier comes from a long line of film-makers and actors dating back to the earliest days of Spanish cinema. Acting is really in his blood and he made his first film appearance at the age of six.

Despite this, Javier didn't think he would go into the family business, preferring painting, which he studied for four years. He took acting jobs to sustain his career as a painter, but eventually abandoned it.

It was his role in *Jámon Jámon* (1992) which he starred in alongside his future wife Penélope Cruz – strong contender for hottest couple in the world – that secured him international recognition. His talent was noticed in the English-speaking world, but he turned down the initial roles he was offered, feeling his English wasn't yet good enough.

Recognition flooded in with his role in *Before Night Falls* (2000) including from his idol Al Pacino. The movie made him the first Spaniard to receive a nomination for the Academy Award for Best Actor.

His most iconic role is probably the sociopathic assassin he played in *No Country for Old Men* (2007), and this performance saw that he won the Academy Award for

Best Actor – becoming the first Spaniard to do so. Bardem is seen as the new age Robert De Niro, Al Pacino and Jack Nicholson – being completely terrifying in the villains he depicts.

His career today is well established, and his roles have made him a mainstay in Hollywood. From hit films such as *Skyfall* (2012) to the live-action remake of *The Little Mermaid* (2023) Javier continues to electrify us on screen, his machismo undeniable and charisma unbelievable.

He is also the ambassador of Greenpeace for the protection of Antarctica and a strong supporter of LGBTQ+ rights. He's a good man, Savannah.

'I've always said I don't believe in God, I believe in Al Pacino.'

DADDY SCORE

Javier Bardem

OVERALL DADDY/ZADDY SCORE	96
ATTAINABILITY	-75
LOVEABLENESS	94
ABILITY TO CHOP LOGS	97
DAD JOKE EXPERTISE	56
LEADERSHIP SKILLS (AIRPORT DAD MODE ACTIVATION)	75
FASHION FORWARDNESS	62

SPECIAL POWER?
Spanish (hot)

Jeffrey Dean Morgan

Jeffrey Dean Morgan is basically Javier Bardem in a different font. That being said, he has amassed accolades all of his own, and as one of *the* hottest representations of an Irish man in film (after Gerard Butler of course, a Daddy we really should have included), we owe him so much.

Jeffrey is an American actor best known for his role as Negan in *The Walking Dead* (2016-2022), and anyone who watched that show *really* watched that show, so you know his fanbase is concrete and unwavering. Jeffrey broke hearts as Denny Duquette in *Grey's Anatomy* (2006-2009) – if you know, you know. But it was his role as the Irish love interest in *P.S. I Love You* (2007) that really made him a defining Daddy for me. Jeffrey has appeared in over twenty-five feature films but most of his work has been in television.

He lives in New York with his wife and children, where he co-owns a sweet shop with our previously featured Daddy, Paul Rudd.

'There's no man, alive or dead, who's going to fault you for living.'

DADDY SCORE

Jeffrey Dean Morgan

OVERALL DADDY/ZADDY SCORE	73
ATTAINABILITY	0
LOVEABLENESS	77
ABILITY TO CHOP LOGS	81
DAD JOKE EXPERTISE	34
LEADERSHIP SKILLS (AIRPORT DAD MODE ACTIVATION)	96
FASHION FORWARDNESS	39

SPECIAL POWER?
Expert in killing zombies. Protection guaranteed

Gong Yoo

Gong Yoo. The man who slapped an international community into stupidity.

A well-known Korean actor born in Busan, he rose to fame in the early 2000s with his breakout role in *The 1st Shop of Coffee Prince* (2007), a romantic comedy that was a hit with Korean drama viewers worldwide.

At the height of his career, he enlisted in the Korean Armed Forces due to the mandatory military conscription, and then slowly built his career in acting once again. Roles in *Silenced* (2011), *Train to Busan* (2016) and *The Age of Shadows* (2016) saw to it that he once again became a key player in the Korean film and TV world. *Train to Busan* was the top-grossing film in Korea in 2016 and broke box office records across Asia.

It was his performance in *Squid Game* that saw the love for Gong Yoo transcend all language barriers, and we eagerly wait for the next series with a hope he will play a more significant role.

'I think (social media) is so scary, I think it's a tool that makes people lonelier.'

DADDY SCORE

Gong Yoo

OVERALL DADDY/ZADDY SCORE	91
ATTAINABILITY	88
LOVEABLENESS	97
ABILITY TO CHOP LOGS	92
DAD JOKE EXPERTISE	25
LEADERSHIP SKILLS (AIRPORT DAD MODE ACTIVATION)	95
FASHION FORWARDNESS	87

SPECIAL POWER?
Slapping

The train that has been speeding you through the countryside of South Korea, slows till it moves at just a trundle. You had spent the past week in Busan, enjoying the beaches, the mountains, and taking a much-needed break from the bustling capital, Seoul, where you have been living and working for the past few months.

Seoul had welcomed you in, just as you were hoping it would, and you have been loving working as a journalist, immersing yourself in the world and culture. Your Korean has come on in leaps and bounds since being thrown into the deep end, and now, instead of tripping and falling from your tongue, the words seem to roll off with ease.

Though the train is slower, you don't feel frustrated or concerned at all. You are in your main character fantasy. Droplets of rain dance across the window while 'About You Now' by the Sugababes plays in your headphones, you catch your reflection and wonder how it's possible that so many millions of other people are out there living their individual lives right at that very moment. There's a word for it actually: *sonder*. You think of how crazy it is that you will never be able to see the world through any other lens than your own. As you drift off into daydreams the train trundles to a stop and you look around the carriage confused.

'Ladies and gentlemen, the signals up ahead have failed and so we have to wait for them to be repaired. This could take up to an hour, I'm afraid.'

There is a chorus of huffs and sighs throughout the carriage. It is at that point you notice the man who has sat diagonally across from you. He must have joined at the last station and you never even noticed. You catch eyes and you feel a deep sense of recognition that you can't quite pinpoint. Not just that, you become violently aware of how handsome this stranger sitting opposite you is and you desperately hope you haven't done anything like pick your nose or drool in your daze.

He smiles sweetly at you and then in a voice as thick and sweet as honey says, 'I'm afraid I've been in this situation before and it's going to be longer than an hour.'

Now you feel frustrated, 'Really?'

'Yes, I'm sorry to say.'

Like it's trying to hit a cue, your stomach rumbles. The man smiles.

'Hungry?'

'Apparently so!'

'It just so happens I have some yakgwa we could share.' He starts rummaging in his bag and brings out a bag of the honey biscuits.

In applause, your stomach grumbles again. You swallow down the nerves that have built talking to this man who looks like he stepped straight out of a romantic comedy. 'Thank you.' You say as you reach for a few biscuits.

'You're not from here are you?' He looks at you inquisitively.

'How can you tell?' you joke. It's plainly obvious you're not Korean, and its greatest curse and blessing is that it prompts almost every other stranger to speak to you. You tell him where you're from and he nods his head, impressed.

'Your Korean is very good.'

Now you laugh, 'That's very kind, but definitely not true.'

The man chuckles with you, 'I wouldn't lie about that! I promise.'

'I don't know you well enough to know that I'm afraid.'

'Well then, let me introduce myself. My name is Gong.'

Gong. You turn the name over in your brain, trying to reach for some memory of this name. Gong's face is not a face you would easily forget. He is one of the most handsome men you have ever seen.

You and Gong fall into an easy back and forth, him teaching you new Korean words and you telling him what brought you to his country, readily scoffing the yakgwa the whole time. Time seems to pass with an ease and any moments of quiet feel comfortable, even pleasurable, as you look at each other and get to know your likes, hates, desires and faults. Bizarrely, you realise you wouldn't want to be anywhere else but right here on this delayed train to Seoul. The tannoy shocks both you and Gong out of the bubble you are in. 'Our apologies again for the delay to this service. The signal is now working again, and we will be arriving in Seoul in ten minutes.'

Your heart drops and you feel gutted. Gong looks equally perturbed as you move swiftly into Seoul's central station, towards your final destination and ultimately, your parting.

As the train stops once again, you look at each other. His eyes framed by thick fluffy eyebrows. You don't want to forget his eyes.

'Well,' he says.

'Well.' You smile back, heart beating.

'I guess I'll see you around.'

Your stomach turns. There was no chance. 'Yep, I guess.'

'It's been a pleasure chatting to you. Stay safe, OK?' He reaches out to shake your hand and you feel crestfallen. *Of course this has just been a normal platonic chat.* You place your hand in his but you are surprised when you feel a slip of paper pass into your hand.

He smoothly winks at you and walks away out of the train, into the sticky heat of a summer in Seoul.

You open up the piece of paper in your hand and let out a small gasp of air. On it, in scrawled handwriting, is a name and a phone number. But it's the name that has shaken you to your core.

Gong Yoo.

All of the recognition and familiarity floods over you at once.

You'd been speaking to Gong Yoo, *the* Gong Yoo.

And he wants to talk to you more.

Lots more.

Kumail Nanjiani

Kumail Ali Nanjiani brings funny and sexy together in the most wonderful fusion.

A Pakistani-American stand-up comedian and actor, Kumail is known for his roles in the HBO comedy series *Silicon Valley* (2014-2019), the romantic comedy *The Big Sick* (2017) and as Kingo in the Marvel film, *Eternals* (2021). In 2018, he was named as one of the most influential people in the world by *Time* magazine and has received numerous accolades for his work including an Academy Award nomination for Best Original Screenplay and multiple nominations for Primetime Emmy Awards.

Kumail grew up in Karachi, Pakistan and moved to the US when he was eighteen to study computer science and philosophy. He later moved to Chicago to pursue stand-up comedy where he made his name on the circuits.

He wrote the romantic comedy *The Big Sick* with his wife, Emily V. Gordon, and they had a podcast together which is exceptionally cute.

'I stay home. It's the best place to be alone. There is hardly any walk-through traffic.'

DADDY SCORE

Kumali Nanjiani

OVERALL DADDY/ZADDY SCORE	65
ATTAINABILITY	0
LOVEABLENESS	89
ABILITY TO CHOP LOGS	93
DAD JOKE EXPERTISE	98
LEADERSHIP SKILLS (AIRPORT DAD MODE ACTIVATION)	55
FASHION FORWARDNESS	57

SPECIAL POWER?
Comedy

Riz Ahmed

Rizwan Ahmed is the edgy guy who you just *know* reads before he goes to sleep and has an old record player somewhere in his house. At the younger end of the Daddy spectrum, at forty years of age, he secures this role through the sheer worldly wisdom he conveys.

Riz Ahmed is a British rapper and actor. The recipient of an Academy Award, a Primetime Emmy Award and has had nominations for two Golden Globe Awards and two BAFTAs. He has blazed the trail for South Asian Muslim actors and has done it with style.

Riz is super smart, a graduate of Oxford University, attaining a degree in PPE, he later went on to study acting at the Royal Central School of Speech and Drama and hasn't looked back since. His roles in *The Road to Guantanamo* (2006), *Shifty* (2008) and *Four Lions* (2010) were all noted, with the latter being one of his most iconic films to date, equally hilarious and heartbreaking. He had his breakout role in *Nightcrawler* (2014) and through his performance in *The Night Of* (2016) he became the first South Asian and Muslim man to win an acting Emmy.

As a rapper, Riz is a member of the Swet Shop Boys, and though his music didn't attain him the same level of commercial success as his acting, it has been critically acclaimed and his feature on the *Hamilton Mixtape* saw him chart the Billboard top 200.

He is the namesake of the Riz Test (similar to the

Bechdel Test), a method to quantify the nature of Muslim representation in film and TV. It really makes sense, as Riz has been candid and outspoken against the stereotyping of Muslims in the media. He has also raised awareness and funds for the Rohingya and Syrian refugee children.

He is happily married to impressive and bestselling American author, Fatima Farheen Mirza, who unbelievably romantically, he randomly met in a café in New York where they jostled over the same laptop plug points – now that is a meet-cute and a half.

'Bandwagons roll through our lives. It's up to you whether you jump on them unquestioningly or jump on them to overturn them and subvert them.'

DADDY SCORE

Riz Ahmed

OVERALL DADDY/ZADDY SCORE	65
ATTAINABILITY	0
LOVEABLENESS	83
ABILITY TO CHOP LOGS	55
DAD JOKE EXPERTISE	76
LEADERSHIP SKILLS (AIRPORT DAD MODE ACTIVATION)	32
FASHION FORWARDNESS	85

SPECIAL POWER?
Lyrical prowess

Michael Ealy

Now if you were to ask for a visual definition of the word 'fine', then an image of this man should surely be what is supplied.

The American actor is well known for his handsome looks and charming personality, and he is most recognisable for his roles in *Barbershop* (2002), *2 Fast 2 Furious* (2003), *Takers* (2010), *Think Like a Man* (2012), *The Perfect Guy* (2015) and *The Intruder* (2019). He has also starred in a number of television series during his acting career. He has been nominated for and won several awards and, over the years, has become an iconic name in Hollywood.

He is married to fellow actor Khatira Rafiqzada and together they have two children.

'I'd love to be able to give to my children what my parents were able to give to me.'

DADDY SCORE

Michael Ealy

OVERALL DADDY/ZADDY SCORE	73
ATTAINABILITY	0
LOVEABLENESS	62
ABILITY TO CHOP LOGS	55
DAD JOKE EXPERTISE	12
LEADERSHIP SKILLS (AIRPORT DAD MODE ACTIVATION)	89
FASHION FORWARDNESS	21

SPECIAL POWER?
Those eyes, those eyes are powerful

Stanley Tucci

Ah, Stanley Tucci, the people's Daddy. The supreme representative for bald men of the world.

Stanley was born in New York to an Italian-American family who are artists by trade. His desire to try acting started in high school and he made his film debut in 1985. He continued to play supporting roles throughout his younger years (search 'Stanley Tucci young' for your own research).

He ascend to stardom in *Road to Perdition* (2002), *The Terminal* (2004) and the iconic *The Devil Wears Prada* (2006). He was nominated for an Academy Award for his spine-chilling performance in *The Lovely Bones* (2009). I don't think anyone has as diverse an acting profile! Whether you loved him in *Burlesque* (2010), *Easy A* (2010), *Captain America* (2011), *The Hunger Games* series (2012-2015), *Spotlight* (2015), *Supernova* (2020) or *Worth* (2020), one thing is for sure: Mr Tucci stays booked and busy. He has an extensive career behind the camera as director on multiple films, and is also beloved for curating delicious food and drink for his TV show. A supporter of many good causes including the UNHCR, and is a bestselling author to boot.

'I would rather just do the things I want to do.'

DADDY SCORE

Stanley Tucci

OVERALL DADDY/ZADDY SCORE	87
ATTAINABILITY	-100
LOVEABLENESS	100
ABILITY TO CHOP LOGS	69
DAD JOKE EXPERTISE	76
LEADERSHIP SKILLS (AIRPORT DAD MODE ACTIVATION)	72
FASHION FORWARDNESS	83

SPECIAL POWER?
Cooking skills

The bustling coffee shop meets wine bar is nestled in a corner of West London where everything is double the price it needs to be. A peaceful space, it's a spot that draws in the wealthy and high-profile people from the areas around it.

On this day, you are sat among the eclectic mix of patrons, sipping at your cappuccino while you try to write the first draft of your second novel. While you are trying to call forth some dialogue that will move your plot along, staring intently at your laptop screen, your table is knocked, and your cappuccino is sent flying. Thankfully, the spill misses your laptop, but sadly it manages to splash across the bright white shirt you're wearing.

As you huff, assessing the damage, you hear a man with an American lilt say, 'I'm so sorry!'

You look up, about to tell this man where to stick his sorry and you are completely flummoxed to see Stanley Tucci standing before you, his expressive face fixed into a clear apology.

All you can manage is an, 'Oh.'

'Let me buy you another one, and I can give you money for a new shirt too, it's not a problem.' His flamboyancy comes through in his hand gestures, and he seems genuinely concerned for your well-being.

'It's OK,' you finally muster. 'A coffee would be great though, I'm in need of the caffeine today.'

The smile that spreads across his face is completely electric, and immediately you understand why he is a Hollywood darling and a fan favourite, it makes you a bit unsteady on your rickety chair.

He nods and goes to procure you the coffee while you do your best to mop up the damage of the last one.

Though you had been determined to not get distracted, your mind keeps turning to Stanley. The care that exudes from his every pore, the deep interest in his eyes . . . you dismiss it, understanding that this would just be a chance encounter and he would soon be on his merry way.

When he arrives back and places two coffees on the table, you raise your eyebrows in surprise.

'May I?' he asks.

You nod nervously, 'Of course.'

'I'm Stanley.'

You grin. *How could I not know who you are?*

His eyes glimmer as he sips his drink. 'Why are you in need of so much caffeine?'

You close your laptop screen. 'I'm working on my new novel.'

His interest is piqued. 'Is that right?'

'It's my second one. And no matter how hard my brain seems to work, I just can't find the inspiration.'

He leans back and considers you. His eyes dance over your hair that is scraped back, your face that is lightly made up and the mess of a would-be white shirt. You suddenly feel self-conscious.

Stanley looks contemplative. 'What's your name, if you don't mind me asking?'

You tell him, and his eyes widen, 'I read your first book! It was completely brilliant.'

Shock hits you. *This is not real life.* 'You did *not*!'

He laughs, 'I did. I loved it, the way you brought that historical world to life was unbelievably brilliant. It was inspiring for me when I was writing my memoir, made me want to push my writing further. I'm so happy to meet you, I'd been eager to reach out.'

You both chuckle nervously, each as starstruck and exhilarated as the other. The bustle of the coffee shop seems to melt away into the background as you focus entirely on each other. Time takes a pause to allow you both to appreciate a connection sprung out of nothing.

'I'd love to ask you more about it, if you'd be able to spare the time.'

A feeling of ease and comfort envelops your soul as the conversation starts to spill from you both, back and forth until hours have passed. By the end you feel lighter and more understood than you have in months.

When Stanley does eventually decide to get up to go, he takes a long look at you before saying, 'The universe seemed to want us to meet today.' He lightly places his hand on yours and you feel the roughness of his calluses. He is so close you can smell his rich aftershave. 'I'm glad we did,' he says quietly, before leaving you alone in this quiet corner of West London.

You open your laptop again and look at the blank word document that had been mocking and provoking you just hours before. You breathe deeply, and all of a sudden, but also not surprisingly at all, you know exactly what to write.

Jon Hamm

Jonathan Daniel Hamm is best known for playing the toxic male arsehole and my god does he play the role well. In real life, it's been said he is a really nice guy who was once a teacher before he decided to pursue his dreams, against the odds.

And he's accomplished those dreams and then some. Best known for his role as Don Draper in *Mad Men* (2007-2015) for which he won a Golden Globe, two Screen Actors Guild Awards and a Primetime Emmy, he has also been a major player in film with roles in *Stolen* (2009), *Million Dollar Arm* (2014), *Bridesmaids* (2011), *Baby Driver* (2017) and *Top Gun: Maverick* (2022). He has also voiced roles in animated films including *Shrek Forever After* (2010) and *Minions* (2015).

He is considered to be a sex symbol and has been dubbed the sexiest man alive by various media outlets. Imagine having a biography that says that? I'd be completely insufferable.

'[To aspiring actors] I would say, "Don't be afraid to fail." It's not the end of the world, and in many ways, it's the first step toward learning something and getting better at it.'

DADDY SCORE

Jon Hamm›

OVERALL DADDY/ZADDY SCORE	94
ATTAINABILITY	0
LOVEABLENESS	80
ABILITY TO CHOP LOGS	88
DAD JOKE EXPERTISE	92
LEADERSHIP SKILLS (AIRPORT DAD MODE ACTIVATION)	94
FASHION FORWARDNESS	73

SPECIAL POWER?
Could call you a name and you'd say thank you

Conclusion

So, who is the defining Daddy of today? Who is the ultimate winner of this chaotic and unhinged Top Trumps? Whom, out of these manly darlings, takes that shining award?

Drum roll please . . .

Our top three are:

THIRD PLACE. Pedro Pascal. He couldn't be featured in the subtitle and pride of place on the front cover and not be in the top three. The Daddy who has led an internet trend for more than a year, who, arguably, placed Daddies on the map, we thank you.

SECOND PLACE. Ryan Gosling. He's Kenough for us. The goofy, silly Labrador Retriever guys win this battle. When he wore his wife's initial as a necklace to the *Barbie* premiere, we knew that he was a man who loves deeply and, though that love can never reach us, we're grateful it exists in this world.

FIRST PLACE. Dwayne 'The Rock' Johnson. He wasn't cast as a demi-god for no reason. A god amongst men, a founding father and a mountain many will never climb. I dub thee, the Zaddy of all Daddies.

And there you have it. I will say now that the scoring that has taken place here has been completely and inarguably biased, based entirely on my own thoughts and opinions. This book is a dictatorship, I'm afraid, but I actively encourage you to score these Daddies in your own time and see who your top three are for no other reason than it's pretty fun. Once again, I'd like to thank these men for being the inspiration for abundant fantasies and my hope is that, more than anything, they will be flattered by their inclusion in this book.

I hope the stories here have spiced up your life. All of us want to be told we're not like other girls, to be different from the rest and identified as someone special in the crowd. That's why all of these stories have been written in the second person, because I want anyone to be able to place themselves in these character's shoes and imagine it is happening to them. Whoever you are, you are the central character of your story and you are a magnet of love and kindness. Be empowered to make your own meet-cutes happen in real-life – ask for someone's number, offer a helping hand to someone you have never met before and never hold a compliment back from the people you meet – there are opportunities in this world to be seized and social media doesn't need to be the only way we find connection.

This book has been all about fun, levity and escape, and I hope you will walk away from it with fond memories, renewed crushes and a few laughs. Desire should be something that is celebrated, especially women's passions and desires. Who knows, maybe the more we talk about our fantasies the more men will get a clearer idea of what is sexy and romantic to us. We can only dream.

I leave you with this final message: no matter how unhinged or chaotic your desires might be, how many fancams or fan accounts you make, how many thirst tweets you draft or dreams you have, you never wrote a whole book about Daddies. That was all me.

Fin.

About the Author

This author will not be identifying herself, but needs you to know that she is beautiful, intelligent and a force to be reckoned with. If you saw her on the street, you would undoubtedly double take, she's just that kind of babe. She will not be naming herself for a multitude of reasons, one being that she would probably not be able to look her nan, dad or loving partner in the eyes again. This is also not quite the intellectual work that she was hoping to commence her writing career with, even if it is very much on brand. Mind you, she reckons bell hooks would have loved it.

As a deeply humble person, she doesn't need recognition or fame, but if this book does take off and become a multi-multi-million copy bestseller (in Jesus's name) she will most definitely be doing the big reveal, and her name will be on all further reprints. Editor Beth, please acknowledge.

Here are some entirely made up endorsements to show how great she is:

'Probably the best writer to ever do it' Barack Obama

'The next George Orwell or Virginia Woolf' Stephen King

'Not what I imagined her first book to be' Her university professor

'Greatest author of the twenty-first century' Madonna or Beyoncé

About the Illustrator

Jovilee Burton is a digital illustrator based in London. With a passion for capturing the vibrant essence of pop culture through her artwork, an eye for detail and a love for all things trendy, she creates illustrations that celebrate the icons that are a part of our modern world.

In 2019, she graduated from Leeds Arts University and went on to study Illustration and Visual Media at University of the Arts of London. She has illustrated bold, bright and joyous work with companies such as Bumble, Refinery29, Your Juno, Hachette Publishing Group, Penguin Random House, Waterstones and many more.

You can find her on Instagram @jovilee_illustrations where she'd love to hear from you.